Social Media Marketing

Building a Strong Online Business Presence

(How I Outsmarted the Algorithm and Gained Millions of Followers in Record Time)

William Day

Published By **George Denver**

William Day

Social Media Marketing: Building a Strong Online Business Presence (How I Outsmarted the Algorithm and Gained Millions of Followers in Record Time)

ISBN   978-1-7772636-2-1

No part of this guidebook shall be reproduced in any form without permission in writing from the publisher except in the case of brief quotations embodied in critical articles or reviews.

Legal & Disclaimer

The information contained in this book is not designed to replace or take the place of any form of medicine or professional medical advice. The information in this book has been provided for educational & entertainment purposes only.

The information contained in this book has been compiled from sources deemed reliable, and it is accurate to the best of the Author's knowledge; however, the Author cannot guarantee its accuracy and validity and cannot be held liable for any errors or omissions. Changes are periodically made to this book. You must consult your doctor or get professional medical advice before using any of the suggested remedies, techniques, or information in this book.

Upon using the information contained in this book, you agree to hold harmless the Author from and against any damages, costs, and expenses, including any legal fees potentially resulting from the application of any of the information provided by this guide. This disclaimer applies to any damages or injury caused by the use and application, whether directly or indirectly, of any advice or information presented, whether for breach of contract, tort, negligence, personal injury, criminal intent, or under any other cause of action.

You agree to accept all risks of using the information presented inside this book. You need to consult a professional medical practitioner in order to ensure you are both able and healthy enough to participate in this program.

Table Of Contents

Chapter 1: Social Media Marketing...........1

Chapter 2: Setting Your Social Media Goals 14

Chapter 3: Choosing The Right Social Media Platforms.......................26

Chapter 4: Creating a Compelling Content Strategy.................................43

Chapter 5: Building a Consistent Brand Persona 58

Chapter 6: Understanding Your Target Audience 70

Chapter 7: Leveraging Visual Content for Impact 84

Chapter 8: Digital Marketing Vs Social Media Marketing....................97

Chapter 9: What Is Social Media Manipulate?...112

Chapter 10: Top Social Media Sites To Consider For Your Brand In 2024 136

Chapter 11: How to Check Website Traffic
....159

Chapter 12: How to Apply Social Being
Attentive To Decorate Net Web Page Site
Visitors 168

Chapter 1: Social Media Marketing

Understanding the Importance of Social Media

Social media performs a important characteristic in contemporary interconnected worldwide and has come to be fundamental to many humans's every day lives. Understanding the Importance of social media consists of recognizing its effect on severa additives of society, communique, organization, and private interactions.

Here are some key factors highlighting its significance:

1.   Global Connectivity:

Social media lets in immediately communication and connectivity within the route of the globe. People can connect to friends, family, and co-people no matter geographical obstacles.

1.   Information Sharing:

It serves as a effective platform for sharing and disseminating information unexpectedly. News, traits, and updates spread fast through social media channels, informing customers about contemporary activities.

1. Communication and Networking:

Social media allows communique and networking on each private and expert stages. Individuals can engage with others, be a part of groups of interest, and build relationships.

1. Business and Marketing:

Social media is a precious commercial employer device to sell their products and services. It offers a rate-powerful way to achieve a sizeable target market, build logo interest, and interact with customers.

1. Educational Opportunities:

Social media structures provide educational content material material material and opportunities for gaining knowledge of. Many organizations and institutions use those structures to proportion knowledge, conduct webinars, and connect to students.

1.   Political and Social Movements:

Social media has done a giant position in political and social actions. It serves as a platform for activism, elevating popularity, and mobilizing manual for numerous causes.

1.   Personal Expression:

Social media allows people to specific themselves, percentage their mind, and show off their creativity. It gives a location for self-expression and identity exploration.

1.   Real-time Interaction:

The actual-time nature of social media fosters instantaneous interaction. Users may also interact in discussions, share opinions, and take part in conversations as sports activities unfold.

1.   Customer Feedback and Service:

Businesses can use social media to accumulate client remarks, deal with problems, and offer customer service. This direct interaction allows gather acquire as actual with and loyalty.

1. Job Opportunities:

Social media systems, specifically expert networks like LinkedIn, are used for task searching, recruitment, and networking. Individuals can display off their talents and hook up with ability employers or collaborators.

1. Cultural Influence:

Social media affects cultural developments, popularizing mind, fashion, and behaviors. It shapes and reflects societal norms, contributing to the persevering with evolution of life-style.

1. Market Research:

Businesses leverage social media to behavior market studies and collect insights into patron alternatives and conduct. This real-time data lets in corporations make informed alternatives and adapt their techniques.

1.   Entertainment   and   Content Consumption:

Social media systems are essential assets of leisure, imparting numerous content material material material together with movement photos, memes, and stories. Users can discover and consume diverse multimedia content material material tailor-made to their hobbies.

1.   Influencer Marketing:

Influencers on social media systems have grow to be effective voices with the capability to sway evaluations and traits. Brands collaborate with influencers to attain precise motive audiences and sell products or services.

1.   Crowdsourcing and Collaboration:

Social media allows collaboration and crowdsourcing. Businesses can crowdsource ideas, and people can collaborate on responsibilities no matter physical vicinity. Platforms like GitHub, as an example, permit collaborative software software improvement.

1. Crisis Communication:

Social media performs a crucial role in disseminating facts speedy at some point of emergencies or crises. Organizations, governments, and people use the ones systems to offer updates, percentage protection measures, and coordinate comfort efforts.

1. Learning and Skill Development:

Social media systems host numerous educational content material fabric, tutorials, and on-line guides. Users could have a have a look at new competencies, from coding to cooking, through getting access to numerous educational substances.

1. Cultural Exchange:

Social media breaks down cultural barriers, permitting human beings worldwide to percent and appreciate severa views, traditions, and life.

1. Health Awareness and Support:

Social media serves as a platform for raising interest approximately health issues and assisting groups for people going thru precise fitness annoying situations. It additionally can be a supply of facts on healthful lifestyles.

1. Personal Branding:

Social media lets in people to assemble and show off their manufacturers. Professionals can highlight their expertise, achievements, and interests, that can advantage profession development.

1. Feedback and Iteration:

Businesses can get maintain of immediate feedback on services or products thru social media. This feedback loop allows for non-

forestall development and version based on consumer input.

1.   Event Promotion and Participation:

Social media is considerably used for selling events, every on line and offline. Users can discover and participate in sports, conferences, and webinars, expanding their knowledge and networks.

1.   Economic Impact:

Social media contributes to the economic machine with the aid of way of using growing machine opportunities in digital advertising, content material material introduction, management, and greater.

Understanding the multifaceted roles of social media in numerous elements of society lets in people and businesses harness its capability at the same time as being aware about the associated traumatic conditions and obligations.

Overview of Major Social Media Platforms

Here's a pinnacle level view of fundamental social media systems, highlighting their unique features and capabilities:

1.	Facebook:

Description: Founded in 2004, Facebook is a whole social networking platform.

Features: Users can create profiles, connect to pals, and percentage updates, photographs, and motion pix. It moreover helps agencies and pages for companies and businesses.

Audience: Diverse person base throughout age companies, focusing on non-public connections and content material fabric sharing.

1.	Instagram:

Description: Launched in 2010, Instagram is a visible-centric platform focused on sharing images and quick movement images.

Features: Emphasis on seen content material material material, Stories, IGTV, and in recent times delivered Reels for quick-shape video content material fabric cloth. Influencers, agencies, and those substantially use it for emblem merchandising.

1.   Twitter:

Description: Established in 2006, Twitter is a microblogging platform diagnosed for actual-time, short-shape content cloth.

Features: Users percentage tweets with a individual restriction, look at others, and have interaction in conversations. Hashtags play a huge function in content discovery and trending subjects.

1.   LinkedIn:

Description: Launched in 2003, LinkedIn is a expert networking platform.

Features: Focused   on   profession development, customers construct expert profiles, connect to colleagues, be part of companies,   and   percentage   business enterprise-related content. It's extensively used for method looking and business organization networking.

1. Snapchat:

Description: Introduced in 2011, Snapchat is a multimedia messaging app seemed for disappearing content material cloth.

Features: Users percentage snap shots and films with a brief lifespan, Stories for twenty-4-hour content material fabric, and revolutionary AR filters. Popular among more more youthful demographics.

1. YouTube:

Description: Acquired with the useful resource of Google in 2006, YouTube is a video-sharing platform.

Features: Users upload, percent, and comment on movies. It enables severa content cloth genres, which consist of tutorials, vlogs, tune, and extra. It's a powerful tool for content material creators and entrepreneurs.

1. Pinterest:

Description: Launched in 2010, Pinterest is a seen discovery and bookmarking platform.

Features: Users "pin" photos and content to boards, organizing thoughts and inspirations. Popular for DIY duties, recipes, and way of life perception.

1. TikTok:

Description: TikTok is a brief-shape video platform released in China in 2016 as Douyin.

Features: Users create and percentage quick, progressive motion photographs, often set to tune. Known for its set of rules-driven content material cloth discovery and virality.

1. Reddit:

Description: Founded in 2005, Reddit is a social information aggregation and speak platform.

Features: Users put up content material to numerous companies (subreddits), have interaction in discussions, and vote on posts and comments. It covers a great fashion of topics, fostering niche groups.

1.   WhatsApp:

Description: Acquired by means of manner of Facebook in 2014, WhatsApp is a messaging app.

Features: Users deliver textual content messages, make voice and video calls, and percent media Known for forestall-to-stop encryption, making it famous for non-public and group communication.

Chapter 2: Setting Your Social Media Goals

Defining Objectives for Your Brand

Defining desires on your emblem on social media advertising and advertising involves organising smooth and specific goals that align together with your regular commercial employer method. These objectives feature a roadmap to manual your social media efforts and diploma the fulfillment of your campaigns. Here's a breakdown of key steps to correctly define goals to your logo on social media:

1.   Identify Your Business Goals:

Begin thru information your broader industrial organisation goals. Whether it's growing earnings, brand interest, consumer engagement, or launching a cutting-edge product, your social media goals need to at once make a contribution to the ones dreams.

1.   Understand Your Target Audience:

Define the demographics, hobbies, and behaviors of your target market. Your social media desires should align with correctly accomplishing and attractive this particular audience.

1. Choose Relevant Key Performance Indicators (KPIs):

Select KPIs which might be right away tied for your social media goals. These have to embody engagement charges, conversion fees, obtain, impressions, or consumer delight. Tailor your KPIs to suit your particular commercial organization and advertising and marketing and advertising dreams.

1. Establish Measurable Targets:

Set easy and measurable dreams for every intention. Whether it is a percent increase in engagement, a particular variety of recent fans, or a intention conversion charge, having quantifiable goals lets in you to song progress and check the effectiveness of your social media campaigns.

1. Consider the SMART Criteria:

Ensure your goals are Specific, Measurable, Achievable, Relevant, and Time-sure (SMART). This framework lets in in developing realistic and functionality desires that make a contribution to the overall achievement of your social media method.

1. Align with Brand Identity and Values:

Your social media desires should align in conjunction with your emblem's identity and values. Whether constructing a network, showcasing authenticity, or selling sustainability, ensure that your social media activities reflect and make more potent your brand's photograph.

1. Create a Content Strategy:

Develop a content material material method that enables your social media goals. This includes developing applicable, enticing content that resonates together with your target market and furthers your brand desires.

1. Monitor and Adjust:

Regularly display your social media metrics and check out whether or not or not you meet your goals. If crucial, be organized to adjust your strategy based totally on the records and insights to procure. Social media is dynamic, and versatility is critical to adapting to converting traits and target marketplace behaviors.

1. Integrate Across Channels:

If your brand is lively on a couple of social media systems, ensure that your desires are cohesive at some point of channels. Each platform can also additionally have specific features and target market behaviors, but your regular social media method have to make a contribution to a unified brand message.

1. Continuously Evaluate and Evolve:

Social media landscapes alternate, and so need in your targets. Regularly study the effectiveness of your social media efforts and be inclined to comply your desires to stay consistent with agency traits and shifts in purchaser behavior.

1.   Build Brand Authority and Trust:

Consider goals that concentrate on setting up your logo as an expert in your company. This need to contain sharing idea management content material cloth, collaborating in applicable conversations, and tasty along side your aim market in a sincere and apparent manner.

1.   Encourage User-Generated Content (UGC):

Foster a network round your logo via putting desires related to consumer-generated content material cloth fabric. Encourage your target market to create and percentage content material about your products or services. UGC boosts engagement and serves as real testimonials in your logo.

1.   Optimize for Conversions:

Suppose riding profits is a number one reason; set desires associated with conversion optimization. This should encompass developing click on on-via expenses, improving the conversion fee to your net web page, or the usage of website traffic to unique product pages.

1.   Enhance Customer Support and Satisfaction:

Use social media as a platform to provide outstanding customer service. Set targets for reaction times, choice expenses, and common customer delight. Social media is a precious device for addressing client concerns right now and publicly showcasing your dedication to customer service.

1.   Explore New Audience Segments:

Consider growing your acquire with the useful resource of manner of targeted on new target market segments. Set goals to growth lovers or engagement amongst a selected demographic or geographic place. This method can help diversify your client base and open up new corporation opportunities.

1.   Stay Ahead of Industry Trends:

Include dreams associated with staying beforehand of commercial enterprise employer trends and improvements. Regularly show screen the social media landscape, opposition, and growing era to ensure your emblem stays applicable and at the leading edge of organisation tendencies.

1.   Crisis Management and Reputation Building:

Set goals that specialize in dealing with crises correctly and constructing a extremely good on-line popularity. Establish protocols for managing terrible remarks, addressing controversies, and highlighting terrific factors of your logo to mitigate reputational risks.

1.   Social Listening and Insights:

Make social listening a part of your wants to benefit treasured insights into consumer sentiment, alternatives, and enterprise conversations. This statistics can tell your usual advertising and advertising and marketing approach and help you're making information-driven choices.

1. Collaborate and Partner:

Explore targets associated with collaborations and partnerships with influencers or distinctive manufacturers. This can expand your obtain, beautify credibility, and introduce your emblem to new audiences.

1. Educate and Entertain:

Consider objectives that target teaching and outstanding your goal marketplace. Share informative content material cloth associated with your industry or products and create attractive, shareable content that offers price for your fans' social media enjoy.

SMART Goal Setting for social media

SMART intention placing specially for social media in the context of Social Media Marketing:

1.　　Specific (S): Clearly define the intention you want to collect on social media. Instead of a indistinct aim like "growth engagement," be specific. For instance, "Increase Instagram engagement via 20% inside the subsequent region via higher likes, feedback, and stocks."

2.　　Measurable (M): Establish concrete requirements to tune development. Using the example above, the increase in engagement is measurable via quantitative metrics similar to the good sized form of likes, remarks, and shares. Use analytics tool supplied through social media structures to accumulate this records.

three. Achievable (A): Ensure your social media motive is practical and viable. Consider your modern-day engagement prices, resources, and skills. If your cutting-edge engagement charge is 5%, aiming for a 20%

boom is probably extra manageable than setting an unrealistic purpose like doubling it.

four. Relevant (R): Align your social media reason with broader employer goals. Your social media efforts need to contribute to the general fulfillment of your advertising approach and, consequently, your business organisation desires. For instance, in case your agency objectives to growth brand cognizance, your social media aim may want to in all likelihood reputation on growing your follower depend and acquire.

five. Time-certain (T): Set a ultimate date for accomplishing your social media purpose. This gives a enjoy of urgency and enables you live targeted. Using the earlier instance, you would likely purpose to achieve a 20% boom Instagram engagement within the next three months.

6.   Specific (S):

Specify the unique social media platform or systems you are centered on. For example,

"Increase Twitter engagement" is more unique than a tremendous intention like "Increase social media engagement."

Clearly outline the form of engagement you purpose for likes, feedback, stocks, or click on-throughs.

1. Measurable (M):

Use quantifiable metrics to measure fulfillment. Instead of a indistinct belief of "more lovers," set a specific variety, like "Gain 500 new lovers on Instagram in the next month."

Utilize analytics gear and social media platform insights to music metrics correctly. Measurable desires provide tangible evidence of improvement.

1. Achievable (A):

Assess your property and competencies realistically. If you're a small business with constrained assets, setting a purpose to location up a couple of instances every day on every platform might not be plausible.

Break down big dreams into smaller, possible responsibilities. This makes the general intention seem lots less daunting and could boom the probability of fulfillment.

1.   Relevant (R):

Ensure your social media dreams align together with your time-honored advertising and marketing and advertising technique. If your business business enterprise is launching a today's product, the social media goal may hobby on developing buzz and anticipation through strategic campaigns.

Chapter 3: Choosing The Right Social Media Platforms

In-Depth Analysis of Major Platforms

An in-intensity evaluation of predominant systems in social media advertising and marketing and advertising includes an in depth examination of severa social media structures, their capabilities, target audience demographics, and effectiveness for advertising and marketing and advertising and marketing capabilities. Here, I'll provide insights into three outstanding structures: Facebook, Instagram, and LinkedIn.

Facebook:

1.   Demographics:

Facebook has a sizable purchaser base with severa demographics, making it appropriate for severa businesses.

It is especially famous amongst older age companies, with a big presence of customers aged 30 and above.

1. Advertising Tools:

Facebook gives robust advertising and marketing and advertising gadget, which include centered advertisements, subsidized posts, and carousel commercials.

The platform's focused focused on alternatives allow advertisers to gain particular demographics, hobbies, and behaviors.

1. Engagement and Content Types:

Content on Facebook levels from textual content posts to snap shots, motion photos, and live streams.

The set of guidelines prioritizes content with higher engagement, making it vital for marketers to create compelling and shareable content material material material.

Instagram:

1. Visual Content Focus:

Instagram is a distinctly visible platform, emphasizing photo and video content material fabric.

It is in particular famous among greater more youthful demographics, making it suitable for businesses targeted on a youthful target market.

1. Stories and IGTV:

Instagram Stories and IGTV provide opportunities for immersive and lengthy-shape content material.

Businesses can leverage those functions for at the back of-the-scenes content material cloth, product launches, and storytelling.

1. Influencer Marketing:

Instagram is a hub for influencer marketing and advertising and marketing, in which manufacturers collaborate with influencers to obtain a much broader target marketplace.

Influencer partnerships can beautify logo credibility and remember.

LinkedIn:

1.   Professional Networking:

LinkedIn is a professional networking platform great for B2B advertising and focused on specialists.

Content on LinkedIn frequently specializes in business enterprise insights, notion management, and profession-related topics.

1.   Company Pages and LinkedIn Ads:

LinkedIn offers corporation pages for businesses to expose off their services and products.

Sponsored content material fabric fabric and LinkedIn Ads allow centered advertising to experts based totally on undertaking titles, industries, and business company sizes.

1.   B2B Opportunities:

LinkedIn is a precious platform for B2B lead technology and establishing corporation connections.

The platform's enterprise-orientated environment fosters discussions, collaborations, and statistics-sharing.

Overall Considerations:

1. Content Adaptation:

Tailoring content fabric to every platform's strengths is essential. Visual content material cloth flourishes on Instagram, whilst professional and informative content material fits LinkedIn.

1. Audience Insights:

Understanding every platform's top notch demographics allows craft targeted and powerful advertising and advertising and marketing strategies.

1. Adapting to Algorithm Changes:

Staying updated with set of regulations adjustments on every platform is vital for maintaining visibility and engagement.

Twitter:

1. Real-Time Engagement:

Twitter is understood for its real-time nature, making it suitable for timely updates, information, and tendencies.

Hashtags play a massive role in discoverability and engagement.

1. Conciseness and Frequency:

Due to man or woman obstacles, tweets are concise and to the point.

High-frequency posting is commonplace, developing a steady go with the flow of content material fabric.

1. Customer Interaction:

Twitter is an super platform for direct customer interplay and remarks.

Brands often use it for customer service, addressing queries, and constructing a responsive on-line presence.

Pinterest:

1.   Visual Discovery:

Pinterest is a visible discovery platform wherein customers find out and keep thoughts for severa interests.

It's effective for organizations with visually attractive products or services.

1.   Long-Term Engagement:

Pins on Pinterest have an extended lifespan than special structures, contributing to sustained engagement.

Users regularly revisit forums, supplying ongoing visibility.

1.   E-change Integration:

Pinterest has sturdy e-exchange integrations, allowing clients to keep at once through the platform.

Businesses can leverage "Shop the Look" pins and terrific capabilities for direct income.

Comparative Analysis:

1.   Audience Intent:

Understanding client motive is critical. Twitter customers attempting to find real-time statistics, at the same time as Pinterest clients generally have a discovery and making plans mindset.

1.   Visual vs. Textual Focus:

Pinterest is based totally completely cautiously on visuals, making it best for way of life, style, and home-related corporations.

Twitter, however, is greater textual content-centric however embraces multimedia content cloth.

1.   Trending vs. Evergreen Content:

Twitter excels in sharing and engaging with trending subjects, on the same time as Pinterest content has a more evergreen nature, providing prolonged-term visibility.

1.   Community Building:

Twitter fosters short conversations and network constructing thru retweets and replies.

Pinterest communities are built around shared hobbies, and agency forums facilitate collaboration.

Adaptation and Integration:

1. Cross-Platform Strategies:

Businesses frequently integrate techniques during a couple of structures, tailoring content cloth to each at the same time as retaining a cohesive emblem picture.

1. Analytics and Performance Measurement:

Using platform-unique analytics gear allows degree campaigns' effectiveness and understand goal market conduct.

1. Emerging Trends:

Staying abreast of growing traits on every platform is vital for innovating marketing and advertising and advertising and marketing techniques and maintaining relevance.

Selecting Platforms Aligned with Your Goals

Selecting systems aligned along with your goals in social media advertising and advertising consists of cautiously choosing the structures that splendid healthy your business organization targets, audience, and average advertising strategy. Here's a proof:

1. Define Your Objectives:

Before choosing social media systems, genuinely outline your advertising and marketing dreams. These need to encompass logo attention, lead technology, net website online web web page traffic, network constructing, or client engagement. Each platform caters to one in every of a type desires, so know-how your dreams will guide your alternatives.

2. Know Your Target Audience:

Different demographics pick out unique social media structures. Understand your goal market's age, pastimes, and online conduct. For instance, systems like Instagram or TikTok might be appropriate in case your target marketplace is predominantly younger and visually orientated. Platforms like LinkedIn is probably extra powerful if your audience is more professional.

3. Evaluate Platform Features:

Each social media platform gives unique functions and tools. Consider the strengths of each platform and your goals. For instance, Instagram is extremely good for visual content material cloth fabric, Twitter for real-time updates and engagement, and LinkedIn for expert networking. Match the platform's skills collectively collectively together with your advertising and advertising desires.

4. Resource Allocation:

Assess the property (time, price variety, personnel) you can allocate to social media marketing and advertising and advertising. Managing a couple of structures can be aid-large. It's frequently greater powerful to excel on a few systems than to spread yourself skinny all through many. Choose structures that align collectively together with your useful aid abilties.

five. Competitor Analysis:

Analyze in which your competition are lively on social media. Identify which structures are running properly for them and whether or not or no longer gaps or possibilities exist. While it is critical to distinguish your self, knowledge your enterprise's social media panorama can provide treasured insights.

6. Stay Updated on Trends:

Social media inclinations evolve rapidly. Stay informed approximately rising systems and modifications in consumer conduct. Adaptability and incorporating new systems that align at the aspect of your goals can give you a competitive region.

7. Integration with Overall Marketing Strategy:

Ensure that your selected social media systems seamlessly combine collectively together with your common advertising method. Consistency in messaging and branding at some stage in one-of-a-type channels reinforces your emblem identification and allows reap your advertising and marketing objectives.

8. Analytics and Measurement:

Consider the analytics and dimension device furnished with the aid of each platform. Tracking and studying overall performance metrics is critical for refining your technique. Choose systems with strong analytics aligned at the aspect of your key popular typical overall performance signs (KPIs).

nine. Test and Iterate:

Social media is dynamic, and character opportunities can exchange. Consider walking small assessments on first-rate structures to look which of them yield the first-rate outcomes. Regularly evaluation and adapt your approach based totally absolutely on the overall performance statistics and evolving tendencies.

10. Content Suitability:

Assess the type of content material that performs nicely on every platform. Some systems are extra conducive to seen content (Instagram, Pinterest), even as others prioritize text-based updates (Twitter, LinkedIn). Choose systems that align with the content fabric cloth codecs that resonate most along side your target marketplace.

eleven. Geographic Considerations:

If your agency operates particularly geographic areas, consider the recognition of social media structures in the ones regions. Some structures can also have a more potent presence in certain worldwide locations or areas, making them more effective for undertaking community audiences.

12. Community and Engagement:

Evaluate the network and engagement dynamics on each platform. Some social media systems foster sturdy businesses and discussions, at the identical time as others can be extra passive. Choose structures that encourage the quantity of interplay and engagement you looking for in conjunction with your target audience.

13. Advertising Opportunities:

Explore the advertising and marketing alternatives available on every platform. Paid social media marketing and marketing may be a powerful supplement to natural efforts. Choose systems that offer powerful advertising and advertising answers aligned along side your fee variety and dreams.

14. Platform Policies and Trends:

Be aware of the hints and hints of each platform, specially in industries with particular hints (e.G., healthcare, finance). Stay up to date on platform dispositions and set of regulations adjustments to adjust your method because of this.

15. Mobile vs. Desktop Usage:

Consider whether or not your target market in the main accesses social media on cellular gadgets or computers. Some structures are greater cell-centric, and optimizing your content material for the famous tool can enhance man or woman experience.

16. Brand Personality Fit:

Different social media systems have brilliant tones and atmospheres. Choose structures that align collectively in conjunction with your brand's character and values. For example, systems like Twitter or TikTok might be appropriate in case your brand is idea for its humor.

17. Frequency of Posting:

Evaluate the pinnacle-pleasant posting frequency for each platform. Some structures thrive on common updates, at the same time as others require a more strategic and masses much less commonplace method. Align your posting time table with the platform's super practices.

18. Long-Term Viability:

Consider the extended-term viability and balance of every platform. While it's far important to conform to emerging tendencies, making an funding in structures with a solid character base and a validated music record is vital to make certain a sustainable social media technique.

19. Cross-Promotion Opportunities:

Explore possibilities for move-promoting among structures. Integrating social media efforts all through more than one structures can amplify your achieve and engagement. Choose systems that complement each one of a kind in terms of content material material and target audience.

Chapter 4: Creating A Compelling Content Strategy

Developing Engaging Content Ideas

Developing appealing content cloth material for social media advertising and marketing and advertising and advertising is essential to seize your goal marketplace's attention and stress extraordinary interactions. Here are some glowing thoughts to create compelling content cloth for your social media advertising and marketing approach:

1.   Interactive Polls and Surveys: Conduct polls or surveys on trending topics internal your industry or associated with your merchandise/offerings. Encourage your goal market to proportion their opinions and evaluations. This no longer most effective engages your goal marketplace but also gives treasured insights.

2.   Behind-the-Scenes Sneak Peeks: Take your goal market backstage of your industrial corporation or current method. Share glimpses of the normal operations, crew

43

sports sports, or the making of your merchandise. This lets in humanize your logo and construct a stronger connection with your target audience.

3. User-Generated Content (UGC) Campaigns: Encourage your fans to create content material associated with your emblem and percentage it the usage of a particular hashtag. Highlight and repost the exceptional submissions. UGC gives a easy angle and includes your community in your logo narrative.

4. Visual Storytelling with Carousels: Create visually appealing carousels to inform a story or offer a step-via manner of way of-step guide. Carousels will let you percent greater statistics in a visually enticing layout, maintaining your target market swiping via and spending greater time for your content material.

five. Caption Contests: Post an exciting photograph and invite your followers to create contemporary captions. This sparks creativity and humor amongst your target marketplace, encouraging them to participate and proportion their wit.

6.   Challenges and Competitions: Launch disturbing situations or competitions associated with your region of hobby. It can be a photograph challenge, a dance assignment, or any interest that aligns along side your logo. Offer incentives together with discounts or wonderful content cloth material for individuals.

7.   Educational Content Series: Develop educational content material cloth cloth that offers fee in your goal marketplace. This might be through guidelines, tutorials, or informative pics. Position your brand as an professional for your commercial enterprise enterprise with the aid of using sharing treasured information.

eight. Live Q&A Sessions: Host live query-and-answer instructions in which your target audience can also have interaction with you in actual time. This now not most effective fosters direct conversation but moreover helps cope with problems and collect take delivery of as real with.

nine. Themed Days or Weeks: Create themed content material fabric round unique days or maybe weeks, which consist of holidays, consciousness weeks, or a laugh, unofficial vacations. This allows you to align your content material with modern events and trends.

10. Embrace Memes and Humor: Incorporate humor and memes into your content material cloth cloth, but make sure it aligns at the side of your logo identification. Humorous content material cloth tends to be more shareable and can help your brand resonate with a much wider goal marketplace.

eleven. Infographics and Data Visualizations: Communicate complex statistics or records visually appealingly. Create infographics or statistics visualizations to percent company insights, tendencies, or thrilling information. This makes your content cloth greater shareable and digestible.

12. Themed Contests: Organize contests with topics that resonate together together with your goal market. Contests can generate pride and engagement, whether it's miles a image contest related to your merchandise or a revolutionary undertaking tied to a selected problem.

thirteen. Flashback and Throwback Content: Share nostalgic content material out of your business organisation corporation's facts or enterprise inclinations. This showcases your journey and taps into humans's emotional connection with reminiscing.

14. Collaborations with Influencers: Partner with influencers or organisation specialists to create content material material. Their endorsement and acquire can introduce your logo to a miles broader target market. It's important to pick out influencers

whose values align collectively collectively along with your brand.

15.   Day-in-the-Life   Takeovers: Allow someone out of your crew or an influencer to take over your social media every day. This gives your target audience a unique mindset and gives variety on your content material material fabric.

sixteen.   Interactive Quizzes and Trivia: Develop quizzes or trivia related to your agency or merchandise. This shape of content fabric engages your target audience and educates them in a amusing manner. Share the consequences and inspire participants to proportion their scores.

17.   Seasonal   and   Holiday   Campaigns: Tailor your content cloth to unique seasons or vacations. Create campaigns spherical festive activities, tying your products or services with the holiday spirit. This allows your logo live applicable and well timed.

18.   Customer Spotlights and Testimonials: Showcase your customers via using providing their achievement tales or testimonials. This builds consider and offers social proof of the fee of your products or services.

19.   360-Degree Videos or Virtual Tours: Use 360-degree movies or virtual excursions to present your goal market an immersive experience. This is specially effective for showcasing bodily areas, merchandise, or activities.

20.   Mood Boards and Inspiration: Share temper boards or notion forums that replicate your logo's aesthetic or the innovative manner inside the decrease back of your products. This showcases your brand's fashion and gives content material that your target market can also discover visually appealing.

Remember to test with remarkable content material cloth material codecs and examine the overall overall performance metrics to apprehend what resonates great on the aspect of your target market. Social media is dynamic, so staying adaptable and revolutionary is prime to a a success method.

Crafting a Content Calendar

Crafting a content material fabric fabric calendar is a crucial aspect of effective social media advertising and marketing. It includes planning and scheduling your social media posts in advance to ensure a regular and cohesive on line presence. Here's a breakdown of the method:

1. Define Goals and Audience:

Identify your social media advertising dreams, whether it's miles increasing emblem recognition, the usage of internet website on line traffic, or boosting engagement.

Clearly define your target audience to tailor content material material fabric that resonates with them.

2. Choose Platforms:

Select the social media structures that align together together with your desires and aim marketplace. Each platform has its demographics and engagement patterns.

three. Content Categories:

Determine the kinds of content fabric fabric you want to percentage, which consist of educational posts, promotional content, character-generated content material cloth, or in the again of-the-scenes glimpses.

four. Frequency and Timing:

Decide how frequently you can placed up on every platform. Consistency is key however may range based totally on the platform and your audience.

Consider pinnacle-rated posting instances for each platform, considering time zones and pinnacle engagement durations.

5. Content Mix:

Create numerous content material types, which include pics, movies, infographics, and textual content-primarily based completely posts. Diversifying your content cloth maintains your aim market engaged.

6. Plan:

Develop a monthly or weekly content calendar. Use spreadsheets or devoted social media manage structures to prepare and schedule posts.

7. Align with Events and Holidays:

Incorporate applicable vacations, sports, and business enterprise inclinations into your content material cloth calendar. This lets in keep your content cloth properly timed and relatable.

8. Balance Promotional and Non-Promotional Content:

Maintain a stability among promotional and non-promotional content material material material to avoid overwhelming your goal marketplace with income pitches. Provide rate thru informative or thrilling content cloth material.

9. Engagement Strategy:

Plan engagement strategies at the side of polls, Q&A schooling, and contests to encourage target audience interaction. Respond directly to remarks and messages to foster a enjoy of community.

10. Analytics and Adaptation:

Regularly observe the overall overall performance of your content material using analytics equipment. Track metrics like engagement, achieve, and click on on-through expenses.

Adjust your content material cloth approach based absolutely at the analytics to optimize future posts and campaigns.

eleven. Collaborate and Cross-Promote:

Explore collaborations with influencers or unique manufacturers to increase your achieve.

Cross-sell content fabric during different structures to maximise visibility.

12. Stay Updated:

Keep up with enterprise trends and adjustments in social media algorithms. Adjust your content material fabric cloth calendar and strategies because of this to live relevant.

13. Seasonal and Trend Relevance:

Integrate seasonal issues and trending subjects into your content cloth calendar. This shows that your emblem is contemporary and aware of worldwide activities.

14. User-Generated Content (UGC):

Allocate slots for your calendar for sharing man or woman-generated content. This builds a feel of community and offers real testimonials in your brand.

15. Evergreen Content:

Include evergreen content material material cloth that remains applicable over the years. This can be reused periodically and permits maintain consistency in your messaging.

16. A/B Testing:

Experiment with different content material material codecs, captions, and posting times. Use A/B trying out to find out what resonates incredible collectively along with your target audience and refine your content material approach.

17. Visual Consistency:

Maintain a consistent seen challenge rely at some point of your posts. This may additionally additionally want to include the use of a selected coloration palette, filters, or a recognizable logo aesthetic to decorate brand popularity.

18. Calls-to-Action (CTAs):

Strategically vicinity CTAs for your content cloth cloth to guide customers in the course of favored moves. This may consist of encouraging them to visit your website, sign on for newsletters, or take part in a promoting.

19. Diversity and Inclusivity:

Ensure your content material cloth cloth is numerous and inclusive. Represent exceptional demographics on your visuals and language to make your brand more relatable to a broader target market.

20. Monitoring Competitors:

Keep an eye on your opposition' social media sports sports. Identify a success techniques and include your particular method while studying from their critiques.

21. Content Repurposing:

Maximize the charge of your content material cloth fabric by way of repurposing it at some stage in particular structures or formats. For example, remodel a blog positioned up into an infographic or a video snippet for wider achieve.

22. Social Media Advertising Integration:

If you are going for walks social media advertising and marketing campaigns, align those efforts together along with your natural content fabric calendar for a cohesive and synchronized marketing and advertising approach.

23. Community Engagement:

Actively have interaction at the side of your target audience past truely posting content material cloth. Respond to comments, ask questions, and participate in applicable discussions to foster community round your

Chapter 5: Building A Consistent Brand Persona

Establishing Your Brand's Identity

Establishing your logo's identity on social media advertising and advertising involves developing a amazing and memorable presence that devices your business employer other than others within the digital panorama. This manner is crucial for constructing emblem recognition, fostering purchaser loyalty, and ultimately driving corporation success. Here are key steps to effectively establish your emblem's identity on social media:

1. Define Your Brand Persona: Clearly articulate your emblem's character, values, and voice. Are you amusing and quirky or professional and authoritative? Understanding your emblem persona allows shape the tone of your social media content cloth.

2. Consistent Visual Branding: Use normal visuals, collectively with emblems, color

schemes, and imagery, during all social media structures. A cohesive visible identification enhances brand reputation and reinforces a enjoy of reliability.

three. Craft Compelling Content: Create content that resonates together along with your audience. Tailor your messaging to align along with your brand character, and percent treasured, applicable, and appealing content material cloth that reflects your emblem's values.

4. Choose the Right Platforms: Select social media systems that align in conjunction with your target market and business company dreams. Each platform has a very particular target marketplace and abilities, so tailor your method to maximise your logo's impact.

5. Engage with Your Audience: Actively interact along with your aim marketplace with the aid of way of the use of responding to remarks, messages, and mentions. Building a proper connection with your fanatics fosters a

excessive splendid logo picture and encourages client loyalty.

6. Humanize Your Brand: Showcase the human problem of your logo through introducing the human beings in the returned of it. Share inside the again of-the-scenes content material, employee spotlights, and reminiscences that humanize your logo, making it greater relatable in your audience.

7. Utilize Brand Advocacy: Encourage glad clients and employees to turn out to be logo advocates. User-generated content cloth fabric, testimonials, and endorsements add authenticity on your emblem identification and help assemble receive as true with inner your community.

8. Monitor and Adjust: Regularly display social media analytics to music the general overall performance of your content fabric cloth. Pay interest to what resonates along side your audience and alter your technique consequently. This iterative tool ensures that your brand stays relevant and engaging.

nine. Stay True to Your Values: Consistently communicate and display screen your brand values. Authenticity is essential in building believe, and clients are much more likely to hook up with manufacturers that align with their values.

10. Adapt to Trends: Social media landscapes are dynamic, with inclinations evolving hastily. Stay updated on industry developments and adapt your content method to contain relevant and cutting-edge challenge matters, making sure your emblem stays sparkling and in track with the instances.

11. Create a Content Calendar: Plan your social media content with a content material calendar. This helps keep consistency in posting frequency and ensures that your content material fabric aligns collectively along with your commonplace brand messaging and promotions.

12. Incorporate Storytelling: Narratives have a powerful effect. Use storytelling strategies to percent your brand's journey, milestones, and

fulfillment memories. This personalizes your emblem, making it greater memorable and emotionally resonant collectively together along with your target market.

13. Embrace Visual Storytelling: Leverage the energy of visuals, including snap shots, infographics, and movies, to tell your logo's story. Visual content material material tends to be extra shareable and can supply messages speedy and successfully.

14. Run Contests and Giveaways: Encourage aim market participation by organizing contests and giveaways. This boosts engagement and allows unfold the word about your logo as humans percentage their evaluations together with your products or services.

15. Optimize Your Profiles: Ensure your social media profiles are sincerely optimized. This includes the usage of a steady profile picture, writing compelling and informative bios, and providing hyperlinks for your internet website or one-of-a-kind relevant resources.

16. Collaborate with Influencers: Partner with influencers to your industry to growth your emblem's reach. Influencers can authentically introduce your logo to their fans, offering social evidence and credibility.

17. Monitor Brand Mentions: Keep an eye fixed on social media mentions of your emblem. Address awesome and horrible mentions directly, demonstrating which you are actively engaged and devoted to client delight.

18. Educate and Add Value: Position your emblem as an employer authority with the aid of sharing informative and educational content material cloth. This need to embody how-to publications, agency insights, or hints that upload cost in your target market's lives.

19. Use Humor Thoughtfully: Incorporate humor into your content cloth whilst suitable. Humorous posts could make your emblem greater relatable and shareable, but it's far vital to align the humor at the side of your

logo person and avoid capability misinterpretations.

20. Measure ROI: Set measurable dreams on your social media efforts and regularly inspect your cross again on investment (ROI). Track metrics which includes engagement, follower growth, and conversions to determine the effectiveness of your branding method.

21. Adapt to Algorithm Changes: Social media algorithms regularly evolve. Stay knowledgeable approximately adjustments on systems like Facebook, Instagram, and Twitter, and adjust your method to maximise visibility and engagement in moderate of these adjustments.

22. Promote User Interaction: Encourage customers to proportion their evaluations collectively along with your emblem. User-generated content and testimonials can be effective endorsements, fostering a revel in of community round your brand.

23. Invest in Paid Advertising: Consider allocating a price range for paid social media marketing and advertising to growth your logo's reach. Targeted advertisements let you connect with particular demographics and extend your target market base.

By imposing the ones more strategies, you can in addition refine your brand's identification on social media, construct a committed community, and installation a robust and lasting presence within the virtual vicinity.

Maintaining Consistency Across Platforms

Maintaining consistency across structures in social media advertising and marketing refers to corporations or humans' strategic and cohesive approach to make sure a uniform brand photograph, messaging, and desired online presence all through numerous social media channels. While the idea encourages uniformity, it'd no longer advise replicating the equal data on each platform; instead, it includes adapting content material material

material to in shape each platform's particular characteristics at the identical time as staying actual to the logo identity.

Here's a breakdown of the crucial element factors concerned in retaining consistency across systems in social media advertising and advertising and marketing:

1.   Brand Identity:

Visual Elements: Use regular emblem colorations, fonts, and brand designs throughout all social media structures. This guarantees your target audience can resultseasily recognize and companion your content fabric fabric on the side of your logo.

Tone and Voice: Maintain a steady tone and voice for your messaging. Whether it is a professional, informal, or humorous tone, ensure it aligns together together with your emblem man or woman and resonates collectively together together with your audience.

1.   Adaptation for Each Platform:

Content Tailoring: Customize your content material for each platform. What works on Instagram won't be appropriate for LinkedIn. Understand the goal marketplace and motive of every platform and adapt your content cloth as a end result.

Format Optimization: Adjust content codecs to suit the selections of each platform. For example, Instagram might be more visible, while Twitter may also moreover furthermore require concise and impactful messages interior man or woman limits.

1.   Posting Schedule:

Consistent Posting Times: Establish a normal posting schedule throughout structures. Consistency in posting times allows assemble target audience expectancies and ensures that your content reaches maximum fans.

Frequency: Maintain a stability in the frequency of your posts. Avoid overposting or lengthy periods of inactivity. Consistency in posting frequency allows maintain your target audience engaged.

1.   Engagement and Interactions:

Response Strategy: Develop a steady reaction approach for comments, messages, and mentions. Timely and thoughtful responses make a contribution to a excellent brand picture and purchaser delight.

User-generated Content: Encourage and famend man or woman-generated content material usually. This fosters a enjoy of network and provides authenticity to your emblem.

1.   Analytics and Monitoring:

Performance Analysis: Regularly examine the overall performance of your content cloth material on each platform the use of analytics gear. Adjust your approach based totally completely totally on insights to beautify engagement and accumulate.

Monitoring Trends: Stay up to date on platform-particular tendencies and updates. Adapting to adjustments ensures your content fabric remains applicable and aligned with the platform's evolving dynamics.

1.   Content Themes and Messaging:

Storytelling: Develop regular storytelling troubles that align alongside aspect your emblem narrative. Whether it's miles sharing client achievement memories, inside the back of-the-scenes glimpses, or educational content cloth, keep a narrative thread that runs thru all structures.

Message Alignment: Ensure that your emblem's middle messages and values live constant. Whether you percentage promotional content cloth or address social issues, the overarching message must align along with your emblem ethos.

Chapter 6: Understanding Your Target Audience

Conducting Audience Research

Audience studies are essential in growing an effective social media advertising and marketing technique. This way consists of amassing and reading records about the target audience better to understand their opportunities, behaviors, and needs. Here's a breakdown of the essential detail steps involved in wearing out purpose marketplace studies for social media advertising and marketing:

1.   Define Your Goals: Clearly define the goals of your social media advertising and marketing and marketing advertising campaign. Whether it's far growing emblem awareness, using internet web page internet site on line site visitors, or boosting engagement, records your dreams will assist form your research method.

2.   Identify Target Demographics: Determine the demographics of your aim

market, together with age, gender, vicinity, career, and interests. Social media systems offer valuable demographic insights that may guide your content material fabric cloth approach.

three. Utilize Social Media Analytics: Leverage the analytics equipment provided thru social media systems to accumulate records to your modern aim market. Platforms like Facebook, Instagram, and Twitter offer insights into person demographics, engagement metrics, and content material fabric common overall performance.

4.   Survey Your Audience: Conduct surveys or polls on social media to gather comments from your target market right away. Ask questions about their choices, demanding situations, and what form of content they find maximum treasured. This qualitative statistics can offer deeper insights.

five.   Competitor Analysis: Analyze the social media presence of your opposition. Identify the form of content material they percentage, engagement tiers, and the demographics they aim. This permit you to recognize market gaps and refine your method.

6. Social Listening: Monitor social media conversations approximately your enterprise or brand using social listening gadget. Identify developments, sentiments, and not unusual troubles referred to with the useful useful resource of your audience. This real-time information can inform your content material fabric fabric and engagement approach.

7. Create Buyer Personas: Develop unique customer personas based totally in your research findings. These personas must constitute your ideal customers and embody records approximately their motivations, pain elements, and desired content material types.

eight. Test and Iterate: Implement your social media strategy primarily based at the insights gathered, but be prepared to iterate. Regularly examine widely wide-spread overall overall performance metrics and alter your method to make certain you effectively reap and have interaction your aim marketplace.

nine.   Stay Updated: Social media inclinations and goal market behaviors can evolve all at once. Stay informed approximately enterprise dispositions, platform updates, and changes in intention market alternatives to comply your method for this reason.

10.   Incorporate Multichannel Insights: Consider how your target market behaves throughout social media channels. Each platform has its dynamics, and know-how how your target market interacts on each can help tailor your content fabric for optimum effect.

11.   Explore Influencer Audiences: Analyze the fans of influencers in your organization. Influencers frequently have a committed following, and records their target audience can provide insights into the wider market and functionality patron segments.

12. Engage in Social Media Groups and Forums: Participate in applicable social media companies and forums wherein your goal market will probably present. Observe discussions, perceive commonplace pain elements, and use this qualitative facts to refine your messaging.

thirteen. Track Hashtags and Keywords: Monitor famous hashtags and key terms related to your enterprise. This will assist you to find out trending topics and recognize your target marketplace's language, allowing you to tailor your content material cloth for max relevance.

14. Mobile Behavior Analysis: Consider the cellular conduct of your target marketplace. Many social media customers get right of entry to structures through cell gadgets. Ensure that your content material is optimized for mobile viewing and interplay to meet your audience's alternatives.

15. Segmentation Strategies: Divide your goal market into segments primarily based

mostly on unique criteria together with demographics, behaviors, or alternatives. This permits for greater focused content creation, ensuring that specific segments of your aim marketplace acquire content material that resonates with them.

16. Social Media Surveys and Polls: Use social media abilities like surveys and polls to accumulate remarks on particular subjects. This real-time engagement offers treasured information and enhances your relationship with the audience through using concerning them in choice-making.

17. Cross-Channel Analysis: Evaluate how your aim marketplace engages with one among a type on line channels besides social media. Understand their behavior for your website, weblog, or e-mail campaigns. This holistic technique ensures a entire expertise of your goal marketplace's virtual footprint.

18. Monitor Online Reviews: Keep a watch on on-line reviews and feedback about your logo on social media systems. Address

purchaser comments proper away and use this information to understand areas for development and enhance your brand's outstanding elements.

19.   Time-of-Day Analysis: Determine the maximum active instances to your goal marketplace on social media. Post content fabric cloth at some point of pinnacle hours to maximize visibility and engagement. Platform analytics can provide insights into even as your target marketplace is maximum energetic.

20.   Utilize AI and Machine Learning: Leverage AI and tool learning equipment to analyze large datasets correctly. These technology can help select out patterns, tendencies, and correlations in your goal marketplace information, supplying deeper insights that won't be immediately apparent via manual evaluation.

Remember, goal marketplace research is an ongoing way. Regularly revisit your research techniques, adapt to modifications inside the social media landscape, and stay attuned on your target audience's evolving needs and picks to maintain a a fulfillment and applicable social media advertising approach.

Creating Audience Personas

Creating intention marketplace personas in social media advertising and marketing includes developing unique and semi-fictional representations of your exceptional audience. These personas assist marketers better understand and hook up with their target market, permitting greater powerful and centered social media techniques. Here's a breakdown of the technique:

1.   Research and Data Collection:

Start thru collecting records about your current goal market and capacity customers. Utilize social media analytics, surveys, interviews, and market studies to accumulate insights.

Look into demographics, psychographics, behaviors, interests, and options to comprehensively view your target audience.

1.   Identify Key Characteristics:

Based on the accrued data, grow to be aware about key trends that outline your goal market. These can also include age, gender, region, profits, education, hobbies, and values.

Go beyond fundamental demographics and delve into your audience's motivations, demanding conditions, and aspirations.

1.   Segmentation:

Group your intention marketplace into segments primarily based totally on shared trends. This segmentation helps tailor your social media content cloth to specific corporations, making sure your messages resonate with each segment.

1.   Create Persona Profiles:

Develop individual person profiles representing particular segments of your target marketplace. Give every individual a name, a face (the use of inventory images or illustrations), and an in depth backstory.

Include task titles, stressful situations, goals, favored social media structures, and content material choices in every persona profile.

1.   Empathy and Understanding:

Foster empathy via setting your self inside the footwear of each persona. Understand their desires, pain factors, and motivations. This deep expertise permits you to create content material fabric that during reality resonates collectively with your target audience.

1.   Content Tailoring:

Customize your social media content based totally absolutely at the options of each person. Consider the tone, language, visual factors, and varieties of content material that could attraction maximum to each section.

Align your content material cloth with the great goals and demanding situations of each person.

1.   Personalized Messaging:

Craft custom designed messages that communicate proper now to the troubles and goals of each persona. This centered approach will boom the hazard of engagement and conversions.

Use the language and communication fashion that resonates with each man or woman to create a extra proper connection.

1.   Adapt and Evolve:

Regularly evaluation and update your personas due to the fact the social media panorama and your audience evolve. Stay bendy and modify your techniques primarily based totally on changing dispositions and options.

1.   Platform Preferences:

Understand which social media structures your personas select. Different demographics generally tend to choose out precise systems. For example, greater youthful audiences is probably extra active on structures like Instagram and TikTok, even as experts can also engage extra on LinkedIn. Tailor your content material fabric and advertising and marketing techniques consequently.

1. Device Usage and Accessibility:

Consider the gadgets your audience makes use of to get right of access to social media. Whether they predominantly use smartphones, drugs, or laptop structures can effect the layout and layout of your content fabric cloth. Ensure that your visuals and messages are optimized for the gadgets your personas are most probable to apply.

1. Behavioral Patterns:

Analyze the behavioral patterns of your goal marketplace on social media. Identify pinnacle hobby times, frequency of engagement, and favored content material formats. This statistics permit you to time table posts at superior times and create content fabric that aligns with their on-line behavior.

1.   Influencer Alignment:

Explore the influencers and concept leaders your personas follow. Collaborate with influencers whose values align with the ones of your target audience personas. This can beautify the credibility of your brand and assist you tap into current communities.

1.   Feedback and Iteration:

Encourage feedback out of your target market thru surveys, polls, and feedback. Use this facts to iterate in your personas and refine your social media strategies. Actively taking note of your goal market fosters a experience of community and suggests which you price their reviews.

1.   Lifestyle Integration:

Integrate factors of your intention marketplace's way of lifestyles into your content material material cloth. Understand their each day workouts, pastimes, and pastimes, and infuse those elements into your social media campaigns. This technique makes your brand extra relatable and can create more potent emotional connections.

1.   Cross-Channel Consistency:

Ensure consistency for your messaging and branding during special social media channels. While adapting content material to in form the nuances of each platform, preserve a cohesive brand photo. This allows fortify your brand identity and makes it less difficult for personas to apprehend and have interaction collectively together with your content cloth material.

Chapter 7: Leveraging Visual Content For Impact

Importance of Visuals in Social Media Marketing

Visuals play a pivotal feature in Social Media Marketing (SMM) because of their precise capability to capture interest, bring messages successfully, and decorate engagement. Here are a few awesome additives highlighting the significance of visuals in SMM:

1. First Impressions and Attention Grabbing:

In the fast-paced global of social media, customers scroll through big portions of content. Visually attractive pics and films are much more likely to lure the eye and make a long-lasting first impact.

Strong visuals are a effective device to prevent customers mid-scroll, attractive them to find out the content material cloth similarly. This initial interest is important in a landscape where opposition for person hobby is fierce.

2. Storytelling and Brand Identity:

Visuals are instrumental in conveying the story and character of a emblem. Businesses can installation and guide their brand identification via cautiously curated photographs and motion photographs, fostering a reference to the audience.

Consistent and visually compelling content permits gather logo reputation, making it less difficult for clients to accomplice visuals with a selected emblem or product.

3. Emotional Connection and Engagement:

Visuals can evoke feelings more efficiently than textual content by myself. Emotionally charged photos or movies can create a deeper connection with the target audience, developing engagement and logo loyalty.

Brands frequently leverage visually-pushed storytelling to hook up with their target market in my opinion, growing a revel in of authenticity and relatability.

four. Increased Shareability and Virality:

Visual content fabric material is much more likely to be shared within the direction of social media than text-based totally content material. Eye-catching visuals are inherently shareable, contributing to multiplied obtain and capacity virality.

Shared visuals can fast achieve a broader target marketplace, facilitating natural boom and logo or advertising campaign publicity.

five. Platform-Specific Optimization:

Different social media structures have great options for visible content material. Understanding and optimizing visuals steady with each platform's specs and character conduct complements the effectiveness of SMM efforts.

Tailoring visuals to wholesome the platform's aesthetics and requirements ensures that the content material fabric seamlessly integrates into clients' feeds, maximizing its impact.

6. Visual Search and Discovery:

The upward thrust of visible are seeking on structures like Pinterest and Instagram underscores the importance of pictures inside the on-line discovery approach. Users can find out associated content fabric and products based totally totally on visually similar pics.

Businesses can capitalize in this fashion via the usage of optimizing visuals for seek, growing the probabilities of their merchandise or content being determined by way of the use of customers inquisitive about similar visible aesthetics.

7. Conversion Optimization:

Visuals play a critical characteristic in driving conversions. Visuals can substantially effect someone's preference-making process, whether or no longer it's far an appealing product photo, an infographic showcasing key features, or a video demonstrating product utilization.

Well-crafted visuals can characteristic effective calls to motion, prompting customers to take favored movements inclusive of purchasing, signing up, or downloading content cloth.

eight. Adaptability Across Platforms:

Visual content fabric is versatile and can be tailored to numerous social media structures, every with its particular purpose market and content fabric requirements. Adapting content cloth fabric from Instagram's visually focused feed to Twitter's emphasis on concise visuals guarantees most visibility and engagement in the course of numerous structures.

nine. Search engine optimization and Discoverability:

Visual factors make contributions to seo (seo). Alt text, photograph descriptions, and hashtags related to visuals beautify the discoverability of content no longer excellent on social media systems however moreover thru engines like google like Google.

Optimizing visuals for search engine advertising improves the probabilities of content material cloth being located through customers seeking out related topics or merchandise.

10. User-Generated Content (UGC) Encouragement:

Visuals regularly stimulate consumer-generated content material. Encouraging clients to proportion snap shots or movies related to a brand or product can create a experience of network and authenticity.

UGC serves as social evidence, showcasing real people attractive with a logo, which can effect functionality customers and construct accept as true with.

eleven. Data Visualization and Infographics:

Visuals are effective equipment for presenting complex information concisely and understandably. Infographics, charts, and graphs make records greater digestible and shareable, contributing to the instructional charge of social media content material fabric.

12. Trend Riding and Timely Relevance:

Visual content material fabric lets in manufacturers to conform to and capitalize on traits fast. Whether growing memes, taking part in challenges, or incorporating cutting-edge sports into visuals, manufacturers can stay applicable and resonate with their goal market in actual-time.

13. Mobile-Friendly Engagement:

With a growing quantity of users gaining access to social media on cellular devices, visually appealing content material material is essential for cell-pleasant engagement. Images and movies are extra with out issue ate up on smaller shows, imparting a continuing customer enjoy.

14. Analytics and Performance Tracking:

Visual content fabric often generates rich analytics statistics. Platforms provide insights into metrics which encompass engagement, impressions, and click on-through rates for pics and films, permitting marketers to refine their techniques based on overall performance information.

15. Cultural Relevance and Diversity:

Visuals provide an avenue for expressing cultural relevance and range. Including severa pictures and movies in advertising campaigns displays an inclusive brand and resonates with a far broader target audience, fostering a revel in of example.

Tips for Creating Eye-Catching Graphics and Videos

Creating beautiful pictures and movies for social media marketing is critical for taking pix your target market's hobby and selling engagement. Here are some more pointers to help you stand out:

1. Typography Matters: Integrate innovative and visually appealing typography on your images and motion pictures. Experiment with wonderful fonts, sizes, and patterns to make your textual content factors stand out. Use contrasting shades to decorate clarity.

2. Consistent Branding: Maintain consistency in your branding elements throughout all pix and films. This consists of using the same color palette, logo placement, and visible fashion. Consistency allows in building brand reputation and recall.

3. Interactive Elements: Incorporate interactive elements which embody polls, quizzes, or clickable buttons inner your movement pictures and pics. Encourage your target audience to take part and interact, making the content material cloth extra memorable.

4. Dynamic Animations: Utilize diffused animations or motion images to characteristic a dynamic detail in your visuals. Animated elements can capture interest and engagingly

carry data, making your content cloth fabric greater shareable.

five. Storytelling Techniques: Implement storytelling strategies on your films. Create a story that resonates collectively along with your goal market, making your content material extra relatable and exceptional. Use visible storytelling to awaken feelings and connect to visitors for my part.

6. Quality Imagery and Videos: Invest in super snap shots and movies. Use professional-grade system or rent a professional photographer/videographer to make sure your visuals are sharp, clean, and appealing. Poor first-class can decrease the impact of your message.

7. Play with Colors and Contrast: Experiment with colorful hues and immoderate evaluation to make your photographs pop. Consider the psychology of colors and how they evoke emotions. Choose a colour scheme that aligns collectively along with

your logo and resonates together with your target audience.

eight. Optimize for Mobile: Given the prevalence of cell clients on social media, make certain that your photos and movies are optimized for various cell gadgets. Test extraordinary formats and sizes to assure a seamless viewing revel in throughout shows.

9. Call-to-Action (CTA): Include smooth and compelling calls-to-movement for your visuals. Whether it's far encouraging visitors to like, percent, statement, or go to your website, a well-positioned CTA courses your goal market on the subsequent steps and boosts engagement.

10. Stay Trendy and Relevant: Keep an eye on modern design and content material material tendencies internal your agency and social media structures. Incorporate relevant tendencies to maintain your content clean and appealing for your aim marketplace.

eleven. Custom Illustrations and Icons: Consider incorporating custom illustrations or icons that align together together along with your brand character. Unique visuals can set your content fabric cloth apart and make it greater memorable in your audience.

12. Behind-the-scenes Content: Share in the back of-the-scenes glimpses of your emblem or institution. This offers a human touch to your content material fabric cloth, making it extra relatable and fostering a feel of reference to your aim market.

thirteen. User-Generated Content (UGC): Encourage your target audience to create content material associated with your logo. Feature man or woman-generated content material cloth on your pictures and movies, showcasing the authenticity of your network and building a experience of belonging.

14. 360-Degree Videos and Virtual Reality: Experiment with immersive era like 360-degree movies or virtual reality to provide a completely specific and interactive revel in.

This can be particularly powerful for showcasing merchandise or growing digital excursions.

15. Incorporate Trends and Memes: Stay updated on contemporary social media traits and memes. If suitable on your logo, leverage those trends to create relevant and shareable content. This can increase the risk of your content fabric going viral.

sixteen. Create Tutorials and How-To Videos: Share educational content material via tutorials and the manner-to motion photographs. Whether it is demonstrating product use or presenting beneficial guidelines, this shape of content material fabric is precious and has a tendency to attract engagement.

17. Embrace Minimalism: Sometimes, a high-quality deal less is extra. Embrace minimalistic format requirements to create easy and fashionable pics. A clutter-unfastened visual may be hanging and successfully bring your message.

Chapter 8: Digital Marketing Vs Social Media Marketing

Businesses depend on digital and social media marketing and advertising and marketing techniques to sell their products, offerings, and other styles of services and products. Both of them use the equal social media systems and equipment that allows you to sell their services and products. It isn't always unusual for the advertising and marketing professionals that carry out internet marketing campaigns to have backgrounds and regions of information which can be complimentary to each different. The following differences become apparent to you whilst you study the benefits and downsides of social media advertising and virtual advertising.

1.1What is Digital Marketing?

Learning approximately what digital marketing includes is step one within the route of gaining a draw close to of the versions amongst social media marketing and virtual advertising and advertising and marketing. Any technique for selling services or products on-line that is based on digital era, which includes the internet, is called virtual advertising. A kind of marketing strategies, together with pay-consistent with-click on on advertising, video advertising, associate advertising, and social media advertising, are blanketed in digital advertising and marketing.

1.2 What are Digital Marketing Tools?

When it involves knowledge the versions among social media marketing and virtual advertising and marketing and advertising, digital advertising and marketing machine are in reality vital. It is crucial for cutting-edge digital entrepreneurs to be gift on many forums which will compete with different digital marketers. There are a number of virtual advertising system which could help managers in decreasing the quantity of time they spend on data control and in enhancing the effectiveness of their advertising and advertising method. Listed below are some of the virtual advertising and marketing and advertising gear which can be to be had:

Marketing using social media this is herbal

Marketing through e-mail

Instruments for the manufacturing of content material material

Paid marketing on social media structures

Social media systems and apps

Instruments for storing films

Analytical equipment for internet web sites

seek engine advertising tool

1.3 What is Social Media Marketing?

One of the most massive variations between digital advertising and advertising and marketing and social media advertising and marketing is the fact that social media marketing and advertising is a subset of digital advertising and is finished on severa web websites together with Instagram, Facebook, on the facet of wonderful similar structures. The advent of content material fabric for hundreds of social structures and audiences, interplay with present and potential customers, and the hooked up order of a web presence are all components which is probably often included in social media advertising activities.

1.4 Building Blocks of Social Media Marketing

Comparatively speakme, social media advertising is an essential detail of digital marketing and advertising and marketing and advertising and marketing in location of social media advertising and marketing and advertising and marketing and advertising. When it involves marketing, social media advertising and advertising and advertising and advertising and marketing is a tool this is relatively various and needs robust guiding standards. Within the location of social media management, there are splendid additives that, at the same time as carried out, make contributions to the development of an powerful plan.

1.Four.1Strategy

A plan that has been properly taken into consideration is critical to carrying out fulfillment in social media. It is essential for any social media platform to have tips that dictate what styles of logo identities must be used, what types of content material fabric need to be posted, and what kinds of industrial business company goals must be pursued.

1.Four.2Consistency

When it entails keeping interplay on social media, consistency can be very essential. Make use of automatic structures that allows you to maintain releasing calendars on a month-to-month, weekly, or perhaps each day foundation.

1.Four.3Engagement

In order to display the fulfillment of a brand on social media, it's far important to include social media control software software solutions. The cause of these technology is to display and stay beforehand of the mood and traits within the business enterprise thru monitoring client responses and one of a kind data.

1.Four.4Data and Analytics

It is viable to discover a huge form of evaluation device on social media networks. It is essential to take the facts appreciably and appoint it on the way to evaluate and quantify a selection of factors, which incorporates the efficacy of the efforts, logo reputation, and additional.

1.Four.5Commercial Ads

It is feasible that backed advertisements on social media is probably a exceptionally profitable investment if they may be dealt with efficaciously. Investing in exceptional campaigns that may be customized is the great way to make certain a quality pass decrease again on investment.

1.5 Digital Marketing vs. Social Media Marketing

Each and each digital advertising undertaking necessitates the implementation of social media techniques at the manner to assure prolonged-term involvement and the effective use of marketing strategies. In the occasion that you are thinking about digital advertising and marketing in place of social media advertising, it's far vital to hold in mind the following similarities and contrasts.

Any advertising interest this is done on any and all virtual structures, each offline and online, is considered to be virtual advertising. Although social media advertising is a kind of virtual advertising that is achieved sincerely online and makes use of social media internet web sites, channels, and forums, it is not much like Internet advertising and advertising and advertising.

The goal of digital advertising is often to increase attention by using way of talking with the goal market through a number of contact factors. On the possibility hand, social media advertising and marketing establishes a reference to the purpose market via using social systems.

In order to obtain fulfillment, digital media have to put money into advertisements which might be shown in distinguished venues, which include billboards or tv advertisements. The fulfillment of social media, however, is considerably relying at the content material fabric method this is achieved.

All current styles of advertising and marketing that are based mostly on virtual structures are covered inside the overarching magnificence of virtual media. Because it uses social media interaction platforms, social media marketing is a one-of-a-kind shape of advertising and marketing.

Sales are being predominantly expanded via digital media. A huge type of business goals may be completed through the use of social media, including the examine of competition, the publicity of producers, and different capabilities.

1.6 What Does a Typical Digital Marketing Campaign Include?

When evaluating digital advertising and advertising and marketing and marketing to social media advertising and marketing, it's far no longer viable to have an intensive verbal exchange without additionally discussing virtual marketing duties. Even despite the fact that there are a extraordinary deal of diverse facets to digital marketing, the subsequent are the additives which may be frequently covered in a virtual media advertising marketing campaign.

Use each paid are searching out advertising or search engine optimization (search engine advertising and advertising and marketing) and content technique at the same time as challenge are looking for engine advertising and marketing.

Promotions and campaigns on social media structures, as well as the use of paid advertising and advertising and marketing on Facebook, Instagram, and one-of-a-kind structures, are included inside the elegance of social media promotions.

Promotions for the cell market, collectively with the development of packages and video video games and their published at the Apple Store and Google Play.

Email advertising and marketing refers back to the exercising of selling objects or offerings through using e mail marketing campaigns.

1.7Why Should You Include Social Media Marketing in Your Digital Marketing Campaign?

In present day virtual age, advertising thru social media has evolved into an absolute need to. It is crucial for every business enterprise that desires to increase their target market foreign places and get their logo in front of customers if they want to accumulate those dreams.

When in evaluation to other types of virtual media marketing and advertising, social media advertising and marketing obligations will be inclined to create answers for nearly all of businesses in a greater expedient way. If groups and types want to make the most of the advantages and go back on investment that social media advertising and marketing and advertising offers, they want to embody greater virtual advertising factors into their digital advertising plan similarly to social media advertising and advertising and marketing.

1.8 Which Is More Effective: Social Marketing or Digital Marketing?

When it includes advertising, digital advertising and advertising and social media marketing every have the ability to make tremendous contributions, relying at the goals of a company. In assessment to social media, virtual media has been round for pretty a while. Social media is probably very new.

When it entails advertising, social media marketing has hastily come to be one of the maximum critical manner of advertising for plenty one-of-a-kind styles of businesses. Going in advance, it want to be an crucial part of the advertising plan that is being accomplished. It is ideal for social media and brilliant digital advertising responsibilities to perform in tandem with every different a excellent way to maximise the number of capability clients which is probably efficaciously reached.

1.9 How to Choose Between Digital Marketing and Social Media Marketing?

It is difficult to choose between digital advertising and social media marketing and advertising and marketing, and doing so is not encouraged. Digital marketing is more powerful with the beneficial useful resource of an extended way. On the opportunity hand, there are outstanding characteristics with a view to assist in deciding on each one or both in a manner a good way to make advertising and marketing and advertising greater effective and useful.

1.Nine.1Theoretical Knowledge

There isn't any need for a marketing degree to paintings inside the hassle of virtual or social media advertising and marketing. There are access-stage roles to be had in every of those occupations for the ones who have no previous revel in in advertising and advertising. On the opposite hand, a course that now not excellent teaches the most current-day capabilities inside the discipline however moreover covers all areas of digital advertising and advertising is a lot more useful.

1.Nine.2Personal Interests

A person's desire will determine which of the two advertising and marketing and advertising strategies or careers they select out to pursue. There is a sizeable quantity of room for development in each of those areas, and if you want to pursue each of those career paths, you'll want to demonstrate an interest in records assessment, mission management, performing experiments, checking out hypotheses, and running a collection.

1.Nine.3Career Goals

Marketing thru social media and advertising through digital structures both provide opportunities to growth one's profits and support one's profession. If you boom for your career, there is a extra danger that you may be given the challenge of handling distinctive humans and being given responsibility for the social media or virtual advertising and advertising and marketing technique of your business corporation.

1.10Final Thoughts

It can be essential for a digital advertising and marketing and advertising manager to be knowledgeable approximately the numerous virtual advertising disciplines and that permits you to supervise the execution of a way that assists the business enterprise in engaging in its marketing dreams. However, in evaluation to specific advertising and marketing and marketing and advertising and marketing managers, a social media advertising and marketing and advertising and marketing manager can be accountable for installing, executing, and iterating a organisation's social media technique. Despite this, they'll have a more confined emphasis than exclusive advertising managers. One particular trouble so as to be required of them is that they will have statistics of the severa advertising and marketing and advertising processes and gadget, as well as social media systems. Become an AI-pushed virtual marketer these days through enrolling in our PG Digital Marketing Program, that allows you to educate you approximately all of the devices, strategies, and ideas which is probably associated with virtual advertising and marketing.

Chapter 9: What Is Social Media Manipulate?

When it includes social media, a corporation's presence might also moreover both make and destroy a logo. Posts which are probably scheduled as it must be have the capacity to set up lengthy-lasting relationships with the target audience. The manner in which customers see an enterprise can be altered via using innovative images and content. The power of social media manipulates lies on this very aspect.

Over the course of the remaining numerous years, we've seen companies in conjunction with Wendy's, Duolingo, and others successfully garner new enthusiasts and purchasers via the use of their innovative emblem money owed. This fulfillment isn't always a twist of destiny. A social media marketing plan is constructed and maintained the use of a technique that has been meticulously created, and all of this is part of that method. Within the scope of this essay, we're capable of dissect all the moving quantities which might be chargeable for ensuring the seamless operation of those strategies Take use of those foundations of social media control to guide the strategies that your business enterprise uses in an effort to collect a presence that is worthy of being determined at some point of the systems which can be most critical.

2.1Social media control

A non-stop machine that includes the introduction and scheduling of content material with the purpose of growing and cultivating an target audience in some unspecified time in the future of diverse social media structures is called social media control. This applies to, however isn't constrained to the subsequent:

Content method for social media structures

Administration of one's on-line reputation

Management of the network and social packages

Social media operations and strategies which might be paid for

Management of group contributors and their future boom

In addition to developing emblem publicity and keeping up with the most cutting-edge tendencies at the internet, the advantages of handling social media skip properly beyond the ones expectations. Building extra non-public interactions with aim audiences at scale is made viable through the channel, it really is crucial. The don't forget, affinity, and most significantly, loyalty of a logo can be constructed through the rapport this is created on social media.

2.2 Evolution of social media manage

There isn't any static definition of social media manipulate; as an alternative, it is continuously evolving. The responsibilities which can be involved in retaining a emblem account are always changing because structures and inclinations are normally converting. This method that the obligations are constantly converting. Take, for example, the reality that the author economic machine has essentially revolutionized the manner in which we post on social media in a span of an awful lot less than a few years. Conversations have moved from the overall public to the personal sphere due to the proliferation of social messaging, which has caused more intimate relationships amongst people and the organizations that they adore. It has been transformed from an recognition-centered experience proper into a whole-funnel experience because of social trade, which has altered the way business organisation executives technique the channel. The fact that social media is the usage of how clients hook up with corporations is proven by way of the use of those trends, which demonstrates that social media performs an important function in company.

2.3Responsibilities of a supervisor of social media

While social media managers are liable for masses of activities, which includes administrative and organization improvement obligations, they may be also chargeable for devising strategies that preserve and assemble a social presence. Creation of content material, advertising and marketing plans, profession making plans, and reporting on analytics are clearly a number of the subjects that can be to your to-do listing on any given day. To be powerful in a function that is so fluid, you want a tremendous set of capabilities, which can also furthermore embody, however are not restrained to the subsequent:

Cape of converting

The management

Creative spirit

A enjoy of marvel

Methods of being vital

Social media professionals are able to better control the ever-changing necessities of this commercial enterprise corporation-critical channel due to the truth to the combination of these talents.

2.4How to govern social media profiles

The control of social media debts is a career that calls for each artwork and technological understanding. It is possible for your facts to offer you with a amazing revel in of the way to make investments your assets, every in phrases of money and time; however, societal shifts arise very speedy. Tomorrow, the platform that is now producing effects can see a decline. If you want to make sure that you're organized for any limitations that would come your manner, diversifying your community approach is a stable method to do it. If your presence is nicely-maintained within the direction of the social landscape, an set of rules modification on one platform ought to have much less of an effect at the device than if it have been finished on some other internet site.

In conditions like this, having a social media control tool is absolutely vital. There is a superb time funding involved in posting natively in the course of numerous social media debts. This is because of the reality it's miles critical to go into into every social community manually as a way to submit. Once you don't forget the factors of involvement and tracking, it turns into extra than only a complete-time mission. Tools like as Sprout help companies in scaling their social sports activities in a sustainable way. Workflows for publishing permit for customisation based totally absolutely at the network at the same time as moreover reducing hazard. To placed it some other way, whilst your group is going for walks socially natively, best control manipulate turns into plenty more tough.

Using the ones abilties, you will be capable of pass out of the weeds and into the broader

photo for the purpose that they automate and complement the techniques which might be already in area.

2.5Finding your emblem's target market on social

Identifying your target market is vital to the approach of producing content material fabric that has an impact. People who fall inner this class are considered to be a part of the whole addressable marketplace to your logo. Your functionality to increase more powerful message at some point of all your social media websites may be superior in case you 0 in on those specific parents. By asking the subsequent questions, you will be able to higher locate and appeal to the aim demographic in your brand:

Can you inform me approximately your present intention market?

What particular records are they looking for for, and why are they looking for it?

How do they get this information? Where do they pass?

What varieties of cultural occasions and problem topics do they discover thrilling?

Your approach to social media might be fashioned with the aid of the responses you offer to those turns on, consisting of the structures on which you are present, the manner your brand sounds on line, the traits which might be appealing for your goal marketplace, and the manner in which you speak collectively in conjunction with your clients. Understanding your target market isn't always a one-time interest; as an alternative, it's far an ongoing method. It is possible to preserve a mentality that prioritizes the desires of the customer with the aid of using asking those questions on a everyday basis to each yourself and your institution.

2.6Social media content material material material creation

The manufacturing of content material is an crucial issue of dealing with throughout social media structures. Even at the same time as people may additionally cross surfing to their favored social networks to be able to have interaction with their pals and own family, more than one-1/three of them (36.Three% of them) do so on the way to get some element to do. However, however the reality that the competition is fierce, you may make benefit of those unfastened mins to set up lengthy-lasting relationships together together with your goal market. While you're competing for hobby on social media structures, you are not simply up in the direction of direct competition but moreover more additives which can be clamoring for interest. Other sources of records, which include media stores, magazines, and manufacturers, are some element that entrepreneurs need to consider.

Are you looking to amuse the parents which are looking you? Commentary on subjects which may be becoming viral? Is it a network?

Suggestions and advice? There is a huge form of reasons why customers decide to have interaction with companies on social media. In a social international that is generally evolving, it's miles important in your agency to decide wherein it fits an high-quality manner to hold its relevance. Short-shape video is the most attractive shape of in-feed social fabric almost about formats used for those sorts of content material. TikTok's brief climb to recognition became in large element accountable for its upward push to prominence, and it has now improved to all of the primary social structures in a few shape or every other.

Short-form video is an effective approach for shooting the interest of your target audience without forcing them to commit a extremely good amount of their time to the challenge. An method to social media marketing that is diverse, but, takes use of all one-of-a-kind varieties of material. Even even as it may look like overpowering, this is certainly an possibility disguised as a challenge. There are masses of brief-form video snippets, GIFs, textual content quantities, and different kinds of content that may be created with a single live video broadcast. When it consists of social media structures which incorporates Instagram, Twitter, LinkedIn, and TikTok, Sprout uses its See Social Differently podcast to offer content cloth for user-generated content material cloth.

2.7 Team member manage

According to the findings of The Sprout Social IndexTM 2022, extra than eighty-eight percent of entrepreneurs expect growing the dimensions in their organization inside the course of the subsequent years.

Although this type of improvement can be an brilliant opportunity, it does encompass a studying curve that have to be triumph over. Making a willpower to your personal continual growth is likewise a vital step in growing the capacity of your organization.

In order to enhance your social media team, you want to focus on developing the following four abilities:

As you circulate right right into a undertaking that includes managing people, you could find out which you are required to talk greater regularly on behalf of the efforts that your group is supplying. In order to correctly give an explanation for the consequences of your social media management method, it's far essential to have a stable understanding of the manner to build up and look at facts.

Time manage is a totally critical capability to have even as walking remotely or in hybrid environments. The sizeable shape of meetings that need to take location that lets in you to positioned a plan into motion might also swiftly consume your time table. These meetings encompass stand-ups, one-on-ones, assignment kickoffs, and all the others. Schedule certain instances at some point of which you will be concentrated on some difficulty, and ensure to do frequent audits of your meetings.

The capability to each provide and take shipping of feedback that is positive is greater than just a particular talents. As a superpower, it's miles it. An large majority of human beneficial resource executives (89%) are in settlement that non-prevent comments from pals is the vital thing to advanced business organisation results.

The majority of social media workers are required to live on line at some stage in instances of uncertainty, brand crises, and tragedies that get up at some diploma in the globe. When it consists of implementing preventive steps, you have to now not wait till a person is already struggling with burnout. In order to propose on your group, you want ensure that highbrow health is on the center of your talks, every within the direction of the first-rate instances and the terrible instances.

2.8Reputation manipulate

Have you ever taken into consideration growing a buy from a commercial enterprise, first-rate to discover that they have got obtained terrible feedback at the net? Have you made the acquisition which you had envisage to make? On the opposite hand, you aren't the nice one. The findings of a survey accomplished through Bright Local advocate that virtually three percent of customers are inclined to keep in mind doing industrial organization with a organisation that has an average score of stars or lower.

The renovation of one's recognition on social media is an critical issue of social media manipulate that is however often neglected. Although it could now not be taken into consideration one of the key obligations of a social expert, it is very critical for the fulfillment of any and all corporations. In the event which you are new to managing your on-line popularity, the following three pointers could likely feature a manual for your method:

2.Eight.1Ask for reviews with tact

It is not critical with the intention to appearance ahead to reviews to end up to be had on their private. At different instances, all you have to do is inquire. Make contact along with your most devoted customers and strength clients to look whether or not or no longer or now not they might be willing to speak about their tales together along side your product or offerings. It is vital which you simplify the approach as an lousy lot as possible. Through the supply of a specific spark off or template, it is feasible to boost client observe-thru.

2.Eight.2Respond to each the satisfactory and the horrible

According to the findings of the same Bright Local poll , greater than half of of of clients are more inclined to avoid doing commercial organisation with agencies who do not reply to critiques. It is probably hard to reply to damaging opinions, however doing so is an powerful method to illustrate to customers which you are aware about and price their enter.

2.Eight.3Be proactive about danger manage

It's not continuously the case that feedback will arrive via direct routes. Many instances, people also can communicate your corporation on their personal pages without tagging or referencing your logo account. This is taking location as a substitute often. If you need to preserve on pinnacle of the numerous discussions which can be taking vicinity spherical your commercial enterprise corporation and region, a social listening technique can be of remarkable assist. In order to assist an possibility-driven logo reputation management approach that assists you in putting in prolonged-lasting relationships together with your purpose marketplace, you want to make use of a social listening tool together with Sprout's!

2.9Social media control and scheduling gear

Five years in the beyond, it became difficult to effectively manipulate an active social media presence the use of nearby publishing technology. These days, it's miles in reality tough to do to your private. There is a greater quantity of activity on social media calendars than ever earlier than due to the reality that clients are posting statistics, replying to customers, and managing subsidized tasks. In order for organizations to meet the necessities of a current-day social media method, they need to dedicate sources to the acquisition of social media manipulate and scheduling equipment. These devices are able to more than definitely saving time. The following is a listing of the advantages that come with using a social media control tool:

Increased logo publicity thru powerful optimization of put up timings, which delivered about more performance.

Through the consolidation of incoming communications right right into a unmarried vicinity, which allows for shorter reaction times, higher engagement can be done.

Improved analytics that provide a greater entire attitude into the whole achievement of your social approach.

It is possible to enhance your complete marketing and marketing technology stack thru the use of which encompass a social media manipulate software, that could make it less hard to connect the dots concerning the have an effect on that social media has to your organisation.

2.10 Managing a social media calendar

Your content material method for social media have to deliver an reason for the principle issues that manual your e-book time table and how it connects to the targets of your business company. The social media content fabric cloth calendar that you use gives you a more remarkable view of what you're publishing and while you are posting it at some point of all your channels. An perfect state of affairs to your content fabric calendar might be one wherein it could facilitate each employer and ideation. For the cause of determining whether or not or now not you are assembly the content material cloth mix that became defined for your plan, a chook's eye perspective of your coming near near social media postings might be useful.

Take, as an example, the reality that your enterprise enterprise places a strong reputation at the recruitment of exquisite humans. You might also moreover decide whether or not or now not or not you've got were given were given enough industrial employer corporation emblem posts deliberate for the following week or month with the aid of manner of taking a examine the content cloth fabric calendar that you have created in your social media debts. Because of this exposure, it is going to be a whole lot a great deal much less complicated to determine which factor of the textual content want more interest. You can also hire the Calendar Notes characteristic of Sprout to hold tune of potential content material material fabric thoughts. This is a beneficial trace for parents which might be the use of the platform.

2.11Paid social media classified ads

Worry not in case you are considering whether or not or no longer or no longer it is extra useful to depend upon natural or sponsored social media; there may be no want to decide maximum of the 2. Relationships together together with your fanatics that are maintained through the years are supported by way of your natural efforts. Your advertising and marketing plan for social media, but, can assist you in carrying out new clients in a quicker and extra dependable way through the use of centered on. By combining herbal and paid advertising and advertising and advertising and marketing efforts, a organization can ensure that its emblem remains within the main edge of the minds of each its contemporary-day and capacity customers. It is a tremendous deal greater remarkable if you are able to manage them inside the identical patron interface. For example, Sprout offers guide for sponsored social selling and reporting on systems, permitting entrepreneurs to keep a close to eye on how well their campaigns are doing. By doing so, you will be in a function to test that the cash is being spent effectively and, if it isn't, you may be capable of make any required modifications.

2.12Social media network manipulate

Despite the reality that on line companies had been present for quite a while, they've in no manner been extra big than they will be proper now. Take, as an example, the Facebook institution that Canva maintains. Canva Design Circle is home to more than 250,000 clients who're searching out layout steerage from their friends amongst different designers.

It isn't always essential for the talks which might be taking location in the institution to be centered on the product; however, this is not typically the case. Even if they may be now not related to the product, posts have the capability to supply their crew with a critical perception into the necessities of their target marketplace.

The proliferation of agencies together with those and vertical social networks has caused an increase inside the quantity of parents which are deciding on to behavior their online interactions within the confines of private corporations. If you want to preserve a courting with the people who make up your target market, the satisfactory component you could do is offer them with a platform wherein they could installation their very own connections and bring together a social network. A social media community this is lively cannot be built in a unmarried day, just like Rome. It is vital to undertake a methodical and measured method whether or not introducing new programs or putting in a completely new community.

In order to test stress your approach, you have to start thru setting up a beta software program program this is extraordinary to customers which is probably devoted on your brand and energy clients. When you have got placed your rhythm, you will be able to increase the scale of your goal marketplace.

2.13Navigate the converting international of social media control with self notion

The insights and expertise which might be important for groups to understand wherein they in shape inside the cultural environment of in recent times can be acquired via using social media. Maintaining a web presence is simply one of the many capabilities that a effective social media control plan can do. Over the path of many future years, it is able to help a brand in gaining relevance, gaining supporters, and future-proofing itself.

Chapter 10: Top Social Media Sites To Consider For Your Brand In 2024

It is useful to have know-how approximately the most exquisite social media structures which can be now available, no matter whether or now not you are an professional social media marketer, a marketer who's interested in transitioning into social media advertising, or a enterprise proprietor who desires to take advantage of the massive capability that social media currently has. For this reason, you will be able to optimize the gain of your organisation, engage with the excellent humans, and gather your social media desires.

Undoubtedly, the sheer massive sort of clients on the myriad of social networking packages which might be now to be had isn't always the simplest element to endure in thoughts. In addition to this, you need to hold in mind if the social networking internet site on line is appropriate for every you and your employer. Does it adhere to the photograph of your emblem? Does that social media platform have someone base that you need to draw? Which an entire lot of social media channels are you able to maintain concurrently?

After doing research and compiling data on the most popular social networking platforms in 2024, we made matters less difficult for ourselves. While some of them will sound acquainted to you, others can be surprising to you. We advocate that you browse via this list so that it will get further facts approximately the social media packages that is probably useful for your agency. Keep in thoughts that on the way to have a successful brand, you do no longer want to be present on each and each social media platform.

Social media apps and structures for 2024

The significance of the content cloth to groups and authors, further to the quantity of month-to-month energetic clients, is taken into consideration while determining order on our listing.

three.1 Facebook — three.03 billion MAUs

According to Statista, Facebook is the maximum well-known social networking net website, with extra than three billion customers taking part in its activities on a monthly basis. Facebook is utilized by round 37 percentage of the world's population, in line with this size. Facebook Messenger, the direct messaging software program that may be a spin-off of Facebook, has 931 million customers which can be energetic on a month-to-month foundation. If you need to establish a presence on social media, Facebook is a totally secure select due to the fact extra than seven million advertisers often marketplace their enterprise on Facebook, and extra than 2 hundred million organizations, the bulk of which can be small agencies, utilize the tools that Facebook offers.

Due to the reality that the majority material paperwork, collectively with text, photos, video content material, and Stories, feature very well on Facebook, getting began out on Facebook can't be more truthful. On the opportunity hand, the set of regulations that Facebook uses offers precedence to cloth that generates discussions and enormous connections among human beings, particularly people who consist of participants of the family with circle of relatives and friends.

3.2YouTube — 2.Five billion MAUs

On a day by day foundation, clients of YouTube view a thousand million hours of films on the net web site on-line that allows them to percent motion pictures. In addition to being the second one maximum popular social networking app, YouTube is often called the second one most famous are seeking engine, in the lower back of Google, that is YouTube's determine commercial employer organization. Therefore, in case you utilize movement pics to sell your organization, you need to honestly embody YouTube into your advertising technique. Here is a manual that permits you to stroll you via the tool of creating a YouTube channel to your industrial agency.

three.3WhatsApp — 2 billion MAUs

More than one hundred eighty nations are represented through clients of the messaging software known as WhatsApp. WhatsApp come to be first utilized by customers for the reason of sending textual content messages to their closest buddies and own family contributors. WhatsApp have turn out to be the medium thru which people started connecting with organizations over time. Businesses are capable of deliver customer service and talk updates with customers approximately their purchases the usage of WhatsApp agency platform. In the case of massive groups, the WhatsApp Business API is available, on the same time as the WhatsApp Business app is designed mainly for small companies. Considering that WhatsApp is the messaging medium that is used the most, it has the capability to be an super consumer care channel in your corporation.

three.4Instagram — 2 billion MAUs

Instagram, that could be a social networking internet site that makes a speciality of visible content cloth, is an appropriate location to show off your items or offerings via using images or films. The software program lets in clients to share a sizable form of records, which encompass live movement photographs, pictures, films, Stories, and Reels, amongst terrific multimedia codecs. You are capable of set up an Instagram business agency profile as a brand, which gives you get right of entry to to massive facts on your profile and posts, similarly to the capability to plot Instagram posts with the aid of manner of the use of equipment furnished via way of way of 0.33-celebration corporations. Additionally, it's miles an outstanding place to get consumer-generated material from your goal marketplace due to the fact that customers typically positioned up content material and tag high-quality companies.

3.5WeChat — 1.Three billion MAUs

The Chinese generation organization Tencent, it truly is one in every of the most essential in China, launched WeChat within the 365 days 2011. WeChat, similar to WhatsApp and Messenger, have grow to be first mounted as a speak software; however, it has now superior into an all-in-one platform. Users are able to do a variety of factors, which include but not limited to: shopping for on-line, paying payments, shopping for groceries, moving cash, making bookings, booking cabs, and extra.

It is stable to mention that WeChat is the maximum appreciably used social networking utility in China and at some point of Asia. As a stop end result, WeChat is an superb preference to take into account if you are trying to sell your employer in China, in which well-known social networks like as Facebook and X are prohibited. Both the valid WeChat account and WeChat Moments are locations in which you may run commercials. Additionally, there are a outstanding wide fashion of influencers targeted on WeChat that would assist your enterprise in appealing to hundreds and hundreds of Chinese customers.

3.6TikTok — 1.05 billion MAUs

An app that lets in clients to percentage short movement photographs is referred to as TikTok (in China, it's miles known as Douyin). In spite of the truth that it become truly launched in 2017, it has fast emerge as one of the maximum famous programs inside the international and has currently passed Google due to the fact the maximum taken into consideration internet net website online at the net. The software program TikTok gives users the capability to create and percent films which are everywhere from 15 to 60 seconds in length. Additionally, the app offers customers with a big library of sound outcomes, song samples, and filters that can be used to enhance the motion pictures and lead them to more attractive.

You are capable of discover movies which can be associated with nearly any passion, in conjunction with lip-syncs, dancing, and challenges, in addition to do-it-yourself techniques and instructions at the manner to comply with make-up. The age kind of those who use TikTok inside the United States is spherical 47.Four percent. For this cause, TikTok is an amazing social media network in your company to be gift on if the populace you are trying to reap is young.

three.7Telegram — 700 million MAUs

Telegram is a loose chat issuer that may be used on severa gadgets and does now not impose any regulations on the scale of the media files. The save you-to-quit encryption that Telegram gives for all sports, collectively with conversations, organizations, and fabric that is exchanged among human beings, is the feature that gadgets it apart from one-of-a-type messaging apps. Throughout the years, it's been able to entice a greater quantity of clients because of the truth to its emphasis on protection, in particular whilst WhatsApp determined adjustments to its privacy coverage that would permit it to percentage records with its determine organisation, Meta.

Furthermore, further to presenting one-on-one customer support, there are some of first rate strategies that businesses also can use Telegram. By way of example, agencies have the capacity to expand chatbots for the Telegram platform or use the channel functionality of Telegram if you want to broadcast messages to a maximum of hundred,000 people.

3.8Snapchat — 557 million MAUs

Snaps are quick movies and pics which can be exchanged among buddies on Snapchat. Snaps are also known as "snaps." It changed into the catalyst that added approximately the massive adoption of the vertical video format, which later unfold to one of a kind visual social media packages collectively with Instagram and TikTok. On the opportunity hand, it appears that in reality the proliferation of Instagram Stories, mainly, has hampered the development of Snapchat further to the passion of entrepreneurs in utilising Snapchat for his or her businesses in well-known.

Despite this, 69% of youngsters inside the United States record the usage of Snapchat. Therefore, you have to think about utilising the app if the bulk of your goal market is constituted of young adults. In the event that you are not familiar with Snapchat, we propose which you examine our guide for novices to Snapchat. Additionally, in case you are unsure about whether or not Snapchat or Instagram is better in your agency, we have compiled a brief evaluation of the 2 systems for organizations.

three.9Kuaishou — 626 million MAUs

When in comparison to Douyin or TikTok, Kuaishou is a Chinese competitor. Kuaishou, similar to its opposition, offers customers the capability to add sound bites and stickers to pictures or videos, similarly to to superimpose textual content on top of them. Additionally, users have the ability to record lengthier movies or live go with the flow material to their followers on the perfect internet web site on line. Kuaishou is extra popular amongst an older target market than TikTok is, mainly in rural areas of China. This is specifically right in greater a long way flung regions. E-change income is also greater critical to the app than advertising and advertising and marketing coins is to its widespread income.

3.10 Qzone — 600 million MAUs

Qzone is but some different software program utility superior via Tencent this is centered in China and combines social networking and jogging a weblog. It has greater than six hundred million users that are running on a subscription foundation. Within the social media application, clients have the potential to add multimedia files, maintain journals, compose blogs, play video video games, and flow into tune. Users are capable to hook up with their friends, see a circulate of updates, comment on posts, percentage or reply to postings, and alternate their cowl or profile pix, plenty as once they use Facebook.

3.11 Sina Weibo — 584 million MAUs

The time period "Weibo" in Chinese refers to a micro-weblog. Sina Corporation, a Chinese technology organisation, brought Sina Weibo, regularly called Weibo, in 2009. Sina Weibo is a microblogging network that is comparable to Twitter and Instagram. Weibo allows customers to post snap shots, movies, and stories; it additionally allows users to see trending subjects; clients may additionally embody hashtags in their postings; and clients can use the net website online to deliver and get keep of proper now messages.

When as compared to WeChat, Sina Weibo caters to a more youthful population and offers material that is each extra informative and further constant with cutting-edge tendencies. In factor of truth, constant with The New York Times, Weibo is the region to be in case you "need to move viral" in China. Additionally, Weibo permits businesses to set up valid and tested payments, which lets in them to connect to their fans and engage in paid advertising and advertising offerings.

3.12QQ — 574 million MAUs

Tencent delivered QQ to the Chinese marketplace inside the 3 hundred and sixty five days 1999. Prior to the advent of WeChat, the most well-known messaging app in China modified into QQ. QQ permits clients to do a selection of things further to immediately chatting, collectively with decorating their avatars, looking films, playing online video video games, streaming track, shopping for on-line, running a blog, and making payments among different matters.

QQ is still substantially used by extra youthful those who use social media, regardless of the reality that WeChat has emerge as the dominant social media platform in China. Additionally, it's miles implemented in 80 countries and is offered in a exceptional amount of extra languages. You do not need a cellular telephone range to join up for QQ, it's one of the benefits of the use of this issuer. This appeals to greater more youthful individuals who do now not have cellular gadgets but use the laptop model of the internet internet web site. QQ, however, is more well-known among those who within the mean time are hired. QQ's computer messenger is extensively used due to its character-friendliness and its capability to ship files which might be large than 25 megabytes, a feature that WeChat does no longer allow.

three.13X (previously Twitter) — 556 million MAUs

X, a platform that has around 556 million month-to-month lively clients (as of January 2023), extends an invite to a fixed of those who like posting approximately numerous subjects, which includes politics, sports sports sports, amusement, and statistics. What differentiates the platform that end up previously called Twitter from the bulk of diverse social networking net websites is that it locations a great emphasis on actual-time facts, which incorporates subjects which might be occurring and trending in the suggest time, and it does it in most effective 280 characters (140 for Japanese, Korean, and Chinese).

Twitter is used by some of businesses as an opportunity road for client care. It has been suggested thru entrepreneurs on Twitter that Twitter is the platform wherein greater than eighty percent of social customer service queries are made. Additionally, Salesforce refers to Twitter because the "New 1-800 Number for Customer Service for Customers." Be fine to test out our Twitter Tips for Beginners in case you are absolutely starting out on the network. When you have got got a enterprise draw close at the fundamentals, you have got to investigate the 20 hidden techniques to apply superior look for advertising and marketing and advertising and marketing and income respectively.

3.14 Pinterest — 445 million MAUs

Pinterest serves as a one-save you maintain for finding new mind and gadgets, further to for locating proposal online. On Pinterest, customers "pin" pictures that hyperlink to internet net sites, product pages, weblog entries, and particular cloth that can be decided anywhere on the net. Pinterest's man or woman base is seven times more likely to buy subjects that they've pinned, making it an extremely good platform for generating website visitors in your internet site. Fashion, beauty, home and lawn, and do-it-yourself endeavors are some of the maximum well-known topics and themes on the social net web site. Consequently, if your business enterprise is worried in any of these sectors, you need to supply serious interest to the use of Pinterest marketing if you want to growth the quantity of publicity that your organization receives.

3.15 Reddit — 430 million MAUs

Reddit has been mentioned be the "the front web page of the internet" due to the reality that it competencies a whole lot of content material, collectively with movie star "request from me a few thing" (AMA) occasions, in-depth discussions on specialised topics, and contemporary-day occasions. In April 2023, the website noticed spherical 1.7 billion views. There are subreddits, which might be essentially forums which might be devoted to a tremendous concern rely, for max topics underneath the solar. Therefore, it is a good concept to do studies to decide whether or now not or not there are well-known subreddits that your business employer can be a part of. Subreddits, then again, have varying degrees of involvement. For example, if your agency is a beauty brand, you can benefit from becoming a member of the r/splendor subreddits.

Be privy to the fact that almost all of subreddits do no longer permit self-selling. The cause of this assignment is to engage with clients of the remarkable subreddits through posing and responding to questions, replacing recommendation and assets, and taking factor in conversations. Additionally, further to posting your personal fabric on Reddit and taking aspect in conversations, you can additionally get thoughts for content material and promote it at the platform.

three.16LinkedIn — 424 million MAUs

LinkedIn started as a sincere venture are looking for for engine and resume net website, however it has because of the fact that elevated proper into a expert networking platform wherein industry experts can alternate information, community with one another, and create their non-public manufacturers. The platform now has round 424 million monthly active customers. Additionally, it has superior into an area wherein businesses can perceive themselves as idea leaders of their respective sectors and appeal to the first-rate humans. For the motive of helping you in expanding your LinkedIn Business Page, we have got crafted a sincere 5-step approach. In addition, LinkedIn gives possibilities for marketing, such as the functionality to have tailor-made commercials despatched to the inboxes of clients.

3.17 Twitch — one hundred forty million MAUs

The stay-streaming community Twitch caters especially to game enthusiasts. In addition to various styles of leisure, it affords cloth related to video video video video games. You have the capability to set up a channel, broadcast your video video games, and have interaction in conversation collectively with your audience through the usage of chat. Twitch has superior right proper right into a primary center for the agencies who are concerned in gaming and esports. The suits of a amazing quantity of expert game enthusiasts, organizations, and tournaments are aired on this platform, that is why it's so famous. The network-driven technique that Twitch takes is the number one element within the returned of its achievement. This technique allows content material material manufacturers to cultivate a devoted target market and generate sales thru subscriptions, contributions, and sponsorships.

3.18Tumblr — one hundred thirty five million MAUs

One of the most outstanding social media systems for microblogging, Tumblr has one hundred thirty five million individuals which can be energetic on a month-to-month basis. The material that customers put up can be submitted in a number of office work, collectively with text, snap shots, movies, GIFs, audio samples, links, and additional. Content is shared via users of the net web site on any and all subjects, niches, and pastimes that can be imagined. Additionally, Tumblr gives you the capacity to customize the advent of your blog. Due of this specific purpose, a huge form of human beings select out to make their Tumblr account their internet web site.

three.19Mastodon — 1.7 million MAUs

Mastodon, a pretty extra youthful player within the social media enterprise, noticed a meteoric upward push in recognition in the latter 1/2 of of 2022, going from having three hundred,000 contributors to having over 1.7 million month-to-month energetic clients via manner of the three hundred and sixty five days 2023. Users are succesful to connect with every special thru the use of Mastodon, it really is a decentralized and open-supply application that lets in them to accumulate servers. Users have the capability to make posts which might be as an awful lot as five,000 characters long and embody audio, video, and images.

three.20Bluesky — MAU unknown

Bluesky is a social network that is based totally mostly on an open-deliver protocol and have become designed to be decentralized and invite-excellent. Despite the fact that they've no longer but disclosed their monthly lively character counts to the overall public, the platform reached the milestone of 1,000,000 people in September of 2023. Bluesky changed into evolved through the use of Jack Dorsey, who had formerly served because the CEO of Twitter, whilst he become although in that feature. A top notch similarity can be seen most of the platform and Dorsey's previous supplying, which is also available as separate applications for iOS and android.

Chapter 11: How To Check Website Traffic

It is feasible which you could need to maintain music of the traffic this is coming to your non-public internet website on-line or that of a competitor's net website online. Whether you are attempting to draw new fans or clients, or you are genuinely inquisitive about gaining a higher understanding of the quantity of popularity that your cloth has, there are lots of device that could help you. There are pretty a few techniques that may be used out of your very personal website; however, some of those techniques provide extra of an estimate than a concrete determine. There are exclusive tactics which might be more technical and may not meet your necessities. Gaining the functionality to show your personal on-line traffic in addition to the web page visitors of your combatants may be of exquisite assist to you in ensuring the fulfillment of your business enterprise, irrespective of the professional requirements you've got were given.

4.1 Monitoring Traffic from Your Own Website

Your internet site's statistics may be accessed. It in all fairness simple to have get proper of get right of entry to to to the records of your net net site in case you are using a platform together with WordPress. These skills are blanketed into the net platform to facilitate simple tracking and protection, and they may offer you with an correct photograph of the website online site visitors this is despatched in your net website online.

If you are the usage of WordPress, go to the pinnacle left facet of the precept web page and click on on on Dashboard. You'll discover some of awesome instructions under it.

Click on the My Blogs hyperlink. When you appearance next to the crucial weblog that you have marked, you could see a touch icon with a graph interior of it that is titled Stats. You can also use it to look the entire net page traffic that your net web site gets.

4.1.1Check the sort of weblog publish comments

Examine the whole wide sort of remarks at the weblog article. You may also moreover additionally collect a tough estimate of the sort of people that visit your internet site via searching at the huge type of feedback which might be left on it. This is a clean and fee-free technique. It need to return as no surprise that now not anyone who views your internet web page will depart a declaration. If you're aware of this variety, you'll be capable of more because it need to be estimate the amount of internet web page website site visitors that your net web page receives. On not unusual, spherical one out of each two hundred readers will leave a announcement.

Please go to the "feedback" vicinity of the net website

You will need to manually matter variety range the quantity of remarks if the net internet web page does not offer a listing of them

To get a tough estimate of the range of people who've visited your net page, increase the style of feedback by using the usage of two hundred and multiply the quit give up end result

Please maintain in thoughts that the accuracy of this approach isn't one hundred%. Only for the reason of providing you with a initial estimate, based totally on not unusual probabilities, that is being finished

four.1.2Go on your homepage's video phase

Take a look at the video area of your homepage. You virtually need to go to a video in your internet internet site and click on it so that you can play it when you have covered YouTube or Video into your internet website online. Both YouTube and Vimeo will display the wide kind of perspectives that your video has gotten; but, this is most effective the case if the films were shared publicly. In the event that they will be not, you can no longer be able to decide the quantity of web website online traffic that emerge as passing through the internet internet web page.

If you check the bottom right hand facet of the display, surely under the video display display display screen, you may find out a number of. Your video has had a sure quantity of website online traffic, as verified through way of that huge range.

Please maintain in mind that the fashion of views which are stated does now not continuously equate to the big style of views that definitely stand up. People who clicked on it for a quick time period after which departed are protected in that parent; even though, it ought to offer you with a desired notion of the traffic that your website receives.

4.2Monitoring Traffic Using Plugins and Websites

Make use of Google Analytics. The online website traffic tracking application known as Google Analytics is some of the most extensively used ones presently to be had. This characteristic lets in you to display screen the direction that every visitor located that permits you to get at your net internet site, which could probably help you in figuring out a way to increase your goal marketplace.

There are loose and paid top price codecs to be had for Google Analytics.

A one-of-a-kind tracking huge range may be sent to you after you have got got got correctly registered for Google Analytics. Through the incorporation of that code into your pages, Google can be able to monitor at the same time as your internet internet web page is regarded, who visited your internet website, and the way they decided your web page.

When the use of the traffic tracker, make sure to exclude your non-public net internet web page perspectives using the filtering feature. If you do now not separate your hits from the same old traffic which you get, you can turn out to be with seriously skewed statistics.

There is a fantastic hazard which you visit your internet net web page as an alternative regularly.

The elimination of junk website traffic, which can also moreover in addition distort your findings, is some different essential step that you need to do.

four.2.1Try out Alexa

Alexa is a cloud-based on-line records provider that offers you with entire records about your internet site. A shape of metrics, which include traffic, popularity rankings, demographics reached, internet pace, and further, can be monitored. Although Alexa is not unfastened, the offerings it offers make it viable to get quick and thorough information on the identical time as however being clean to use. Depending on the price range you have available and the requirements of your employer, there are quite a few severa packages available.

It is viable to apply Alexa to reveal not only your private net web website online however additionally the net sites of your combatants. In addition, Alexa is able to offer you with tips which may be primarily based on the traffic data and information of your net web page on-line. Utilizing those suggestions may moreover moreover assist you in enhancing the reach of your web page and attracting a greater style of traffic for your internet website on line.

four.2.2 Keeping tabs with Compete

Comparable to Alexa is the sport Compete. Compete is a tool that assists you in monitoring the site visitors that comes for your net website from humans placed inside the United States. In addition to that, it offers a toolbar that lets in you to right away get right of access to the records of your internet website on line at any second. Competition isn't unfastened, but the internet website online does have lots of club levels to select out out from. There are positive factors which can be protected in each plan that are imagined to assist with any diploma of reporting.

four.3Tracking Competitors' Websites

Determine your fighters within the market. Monitoring the site visitors that comes on your very non-public website is critical; even though, if you really need to make bigger your website, you need moreover keep a watch on the internet web sites which may be competing with you. In the future, it'll probably be useful a good way to make judgments approximately your very very own net website online in case you are privy to the strategies in which a competitor's internet web page isn't always similar to your non-public and the way he communicates along with his intention marketplace. Conduct a are searching out the usage of numerous net search engines like google for the most vital key phrases associated with your website online.

Chapter 12: How To Apply Social Being Attentive To Decorate Net Web Page Site Visitors

Because we stay in a virtual technology, social media has developed into an important issue of our ordinary lives. In addition to this, it has advanced into an critical device for companies who are trying to increase the quantity of site visitors that visits their net web web sites. The exercise of social listening is some of the maximum green techniques for venture this purpose. A method referred to as social listening consists of tracking numerous social media net web websites in order to understand any mentions of your commercial enterprise employer, items, or vicinity. Companies are capable of enhance their on line presence and increase the quantity of site site visitors that visits their internet site through the usage of using social listening, which permits them to accumulate essential insights approximately their intention demographic. In the following paragraphs, we are capable of circulate over the advantages of social listening similarly to the techniques in which it can be used to increase net website online web website visitors.

5.1Understanding social listening and its benefits

First and essential, on the way to use social paying attention to boom internet site web site site visitors, one want to first get an understanding of it. A approach called social listening consists of tracking severa social media websites with a purpose to recognize any mentions of your employer, items, or region. Companies may also beautify their online presence and boom the quantity of internet page traffic that visits their internet internet web page with the useful resource of doing so, which lets in them to acquire crucial insights about their goal marketplace and make use of the ones insights to higher their strategies.

There are a brilliant many advantages to conducting social listening. In the primary place, it gives businesses the functionality to apprehend what their intended purpose marketplace is saying about them on social media. With using this records, the organisation may additionally determine the regions in which it can make upgrades and formulate adjustments which will connect to their goal marketplace. In addition, social listening might also assist corporations in recognizing developments in their respective industries, retaining their competitive aspect, and making well-informed options on their marketing and advertising plans.

The opportunity to speak together with your target market on a more personal diploma is yet each other benefit that includes social listening for businesses. Companies have the ability to reinforce their connections with their target market and enhance their devotion to their brand thru acknowledging and reacting to comments, questions, and criticism. In elegant, social listening is an essential device for agencies that need to increase the quantity of website site visitors that visits their net web sites and enhance their visibility on the net. It is feasible to make knowledgeable judgments which will result in a rise in the amount of website web page traffic that visits your net web page and, in the end, an increase on your bottom line if you have an extensive hold close to of what your target market is pronouncing about your business business enterprise.

five.2Identifying your target marketplace via social listening

When it entails leveraging social listening to growth internet web page website online visitors, one of the most vital steps is to determine who your target market specially is. Companies are capable to expose and observe mentions of their emblem, gadgets, or area on social media structures via using social listening, which may additionally additionally supply them with useful insights about their goal market. When corporations have a smooth draw near of their intention demographic, they are better able to modify their advertising and marketing method and online presence to have a extra impact on accomplishing and attractive with that unique set of people.

Analysis of the demographics of the folks that are referencing your brand on social media is one technique that may be used to decide who your purpose marketplace is thru the usage of social listening practices. A individual's age, gender, area, and pastimes are all examples of this type of records. By doing so, you may have a better understanding of the folks which might be already engaged to your company and the varieties of cloth that connect with them.

Using social listening, you may furthermore decide your audience via way of comparing the sentiment of the mentions of your company. This is yet a few other approach the use of social listening. You may additionally have a better knowledge of ways humans experience approximately your brand and what they cherish due to this. This facts may be used to make bigger messages and campaigns which may be congruent with their beliefs, if you want that will help you in establishing a stronger reference to them.

In large, figuring out your goal market via social listening might also give you with useful statistics that permit you to in tailoring your on-line presence and advertising and marketing techniques to better gain and interact with that unique set of people. You will in the long run be able to improve the amount of traffic that visits your net web page and your bottom line due to this.

five.3Tracking and analyzing mentions of your logo on social media

A exceptional detail of social listening is the monitoring and evaluation of mentions of your business enterprise on severa social media structures. Through the use of this era, companies are capable of show and accumulate records on the severa social media channels on which their emblem is being cited. By using this facts, one might not handiest apprehend styles and trends, however additionally get critical insights on the goal marketplace that they'll be looking to acquire.

A wide style of numerous device and pieces of software program application are available for corporations to apply an top notch way to display and take a look at mentions in their brand on social media systems. With the use of those device, groups are able to set up hashtags and key terms which can be related to their emblem, objects, or area. The application, after it's been configured, will collect facts on all times wherein effective hashtags and phrases are used, and it'll then deliver a complete analysis of the findings.

Information like as the range of mentions, the temper of the factor out, the demographics of the individual that cited the emblem, and the platform wherein the factor out happened may additionally all be protected within the assessment this is supplied through the ones tools. It is possible to utilize this facts to recognize patterns and traits, similarly to to make knowledgeable judgments on a manner to decorate the net presence and advertising and marketing techniques. Firms may additionally additionally moreover beautify their on-line presence, deliver greater visitors to their internet net page, and in the end raise their bottom line through looking and studying mentions in their logo on social media. This allows the businesses to obtain important insights into their target market and appoint the data approximately their target market to enhance their online presence.

five.4Using social taking note of emerge as aware about organisation tendencies and live aggressive

One distinct vital issue of the plan is the use of social listening that allows you to apprehend developments in the market and hold a competitive vicinity. Companies are in a position to show and collect facts on what's being stated approximately their region as well as their fighters on social media thru the exercising of social listening. It is viable to make use of this statistics to apprehend styles and tendencies in the employer, further to to accumulate useful insights into what their opposition are doing nicely and in which they may boom their ordinary usual performance.

Through the monitoring of industry-associated hashtags and key phrases, groups are able to hold a rustic of hobby about the most modern tendencies, items, and services. In order to format new gadgets, services, and advertising strategies which might be consistent with the dispositions which can be presently taking region, this knowledge can be used. A in addition gain of monitoring what humans say about their opposition is that it is able to supply useful insights into what they will be doing well and what they are able to do higher.

One extra technique of use social taking note of maintain a competitive facet is to discover influential people inner your location. Individuals who're seemed as government of their respective fields and who have a brilliant following on social media are known as influencers. Companies are able to find out about the maximum modern traits of their place and discover potential collaborations with the useful resource of searching what they will be pronouncing and hook up with some other.

All topics considered, the usage of social listening as a method of spotting inclinations inside the market and preserving a aggressive location may additionally moreover provide enormous statistics that can help groups in enhancing their on-line presence, attracting more website visitors to their internet site, and ultimately boosting their bottom line. Companies are capable of have interaction in knowledgeable desire-making if you want to assist them in final earlier of the competition in the event that they live knowledgeable approximately the most modern day inclinations and what their opponents are doing.

5.5 Engaging collectively along side your target market through social listening

To efficiently use social being attentive to growth net website site visitors, one of the maximum crucial steps is to engage at the side of your target market through social listening. Not best does social listening allow corporations to preserve tune of what is being stated approximately them on social media, however it furthermore permits them to have interaction with their audience in actual time. Responding to feedback, messages, and direct mentions of your business enterprise, items, or region on social media web sites is one manner to perform this purpose.

Through energetic participation with their target audience, organizations have the opportunity to cultivate connections and earn the trust in their meant target audience. Providing replies which may be both useful and relevant to comments and messages, in addition to making proactive efforts to acquire out to capacity clients, are every approaches in which this can be completed. Companies can also discover common ache elements or issues that get up with the aid of connecting with their target market and then the use of that information to better their goods and services. This is made possible through the engagement of the target audience.

A rise in logo recognition and an increase in the quantity of site visitors that visits your internet net site can also each be accomplished via engagement together with your target marketplace. Through the act of replying to comments, groups have the functionality to elevate the publicity of their logo on social media, which in turn can also moreover result in an increased shape of humans being aware about their brand and journeying their net web website online. In preferred, one of the maximum crucial factors of correctly the usage of the method to increase internet web website site visitors is to actively interact collectively together with your target market via social listening.

Businesses have the capacity to beautify their brand popularity and increase the amount of web page visitors that visits their net internet site with the resource of cultivating connections with their audience and developing bear in thoughts with them. This, in flip, will in the long run enhance their backside line.

five.6Measuring the impact of social listening on internet website visitors

One of the most crucial steps in installing region whether or not or not or not or no longer the approach is successful is to measure the have an effect on that social listening has at the visitors this is travelling the internet site. Businesses are in a position to expose and collect records on what is being stated about them on social media structures thru the workout of social listening. They can then employ this expertise to growth the amount of web page site visitors that visits their internet web page. Nevertheless, it is critical to show and take a look at out the results of those efforts in case you want to verify whether or not or now not or no longer or now not they're generating the results that have been meant.

There are a few amazing strategies to identifying how masses of a electricity social listening has on internet internet web page website online visitors. Recording the amount of visitors to a net website that originate from social media systems is one method. This is a few trouble that may be completed via the use of technologies which incorporates Google Analytics, which gives agencies the capacity to peer the quantity of visits to their internet site in addition to the muse of these website online site traffic. Companies are able to become aware of whether or not or now not their social listening efforts are ensuing in an increase in the amount of website site visitors this is sent to their net web site by means of way of manner of tracking the variety of visits that originate from social media.

The amount of instances your business agency is noted on social media is any other method that can be used to evaluate the impact that social listening has at the web page visitors this is sent for your website. Using software program which includes factor out or Hootsuite, which permit organizations to show mentions of their emblem, goods, or enterprise on social media, is one manner to accomplish this reason. Companies are able to pick out whether or not or not or now not their social listening sports activities are developing brand recognition and essential to an growth internal the quantity of people locating their emblem and visiting their net web site thru the use of monitoring the big style of mentions from their audience.

When it includes putting in place the efficacy of the plan, one of the maximum essential steps is to degree the effect that social listening has on the internet website traffic this is generated by way of using the net website. Companies are capable of compare whether or not they're growing the amount of visitors that visits their website via tracking and comparing the effect of their social listening activities. If they'll be, they're capable of then make changes as critical to enhance their outcomes.

five.7Utilizing social listening equipment and software program program program

One of the maximum critical elements of adopting social taking note of boom internet website visitors is utilising the severa tools and technologies to be had for social listening. Companies are capable to expose and gather records on what's being said approximately them on social media thru using social listening device and software. They can then utilize this statistics to generate greater visitors to their net website on line.

There is a large preference of social listening software program software and system available, each of which has its specific set of talents and functions. Tools like as Hootsuite, Mention, and Brand24 are examples of well-known social listening applications. With using those system, businesses are able to display mentions of their emblem, objects, or region on social media and have interaction with their target market in real time.

The impact of social listening on net website internet website visitors and one of a kind metrics can also be measured through some social listening generation. These structures offer facts on internet website online visits, mentions, and wellknown engagement, which lets in for the scale of the impact of social listening. The functionality of social listening technology to filter and make revel in of the information this is accrued is each other function of these gadget. Some systems are capable of categorize mentions in step with sentiment, troubles, and geography, and they'll even deliver insights at the strategies that opponents are doing.